BIPOLAR
PERSONALITY
DISORDER

*SIGNS, SYMPTOMS, TREATMENTS,
AND HOW TO SURVIVE AND
THRIVE WITH BIPOLAR DISORDER*

BY

GUSTAV FRIEDMAN

TABLE OF CONTENTS

INTRODUCTION

Bipolar ("manic depression") disorder is a mental disorder that is marked by a constantly shifting disposition between depression and mania. The mood is significant, and the experiences of mania and depression are usually extreme. The current attitude can last for several days or even months (see the bipolar depression segment below). A person with this condition usually experiences intense mood swings.

Extreme happiness, hyperactivity, little sleep, and race thoughts, which could lead to fast speech, characterize a manic episode. A depressing episode is characterized by extreme sadness, a lack of energy and interest, a lack of fun, and feelings of helplessness and hopelessness. The average person with a bipolar disorder may have a regular disposition for up to three years of mania or depression.

Bipolar disorder is chronic, which indicates that about 90 percent of people who recover from a single manic episode experience from future episodes. Roughly 70% of psychotic manic episodes arise before or after a depressive episode. Treatment seeks to reduce the mania and depression of the disorder and to restore equilibrium to the mood of the person.

Bipolars often describe their experience as an emotional roller coaster. Riding between strong emotions may prevent a person from getting a "usual" existence. The emotions, thoughts, and behaviors of a person with bipolar disorder often go uncontrolled. Friends, colleagues, and families can sometimes intervene to protect their health and interests. This makes the condition difficult not only for the patient but also for those in contact with him or her.

Through time,the bipolar syndrome can be fast or slow. Those who are cycling quickly are as often as a few times a week between depression and mania (some cycling on the same day). Most people with bipolar disorder are slow-cycling–they experience long periods of upset (high phase) and downset (low phase). Researchers still don't understand why some people cycle faster than others.

Bipolar living can be difficult to maintain a regular lifestyle. Many episodes may contribute to family tensions or financial problems, especially when an individual with bipolar disorder seems to be incorrect and reckless. Often people become impulsive and act aggressively during the manic phase. This can lead to high-risk behaviors, such as repeated poisoning, excessive expenditure, and risky sexual behavior.

Some people with bipolar disorder may experience symptoms in severe manic or depressed events that overwhelm their ability to cope with everyday life and even reality. This failure to distinguish between reality and unreality results in psychotic symptoms such as voices, paranoia, visual hallucinations, and misconceptions of special powers or identity. They may have distressing times of great sorrow and euphoric optimism (a "natural high") and/or rage, which is not typical of the person during wellness periods. Such sudden mood changes conflict with rationality, reasoning, and awareness to a degree such that the affected person may not be conscious of the need for assistance. However, if left untreated, almost all aspects of the life of a person may be seriously affected by bipolar disorder.

Identification and early treatment of the first symptom of mania or depression are important to bipolar disorder recovery. In most cases, there is a depressive episode before a manic episode, and many patients are initially treated as if they have major depression. The first phase of bipolar disorder is typically a depressive period. When a manic episode happens, it becomes clearer that the person has a disease with alternate moods. Due to this diagnostic difficulty, family history of similar disease or episodes is important. Individuals seeking treatment due to a depressed episode may still be treated with unipolar depression until a manic episode develops. Ironically, in some patients, a manic episode may be caused by treating depressed bipolar patients with antidepressants.

HISTORY OF BIPOLAR DISORDER

There is no time like now for bipolar disorder to be diagnosed. Comparisons between what we now know and what we then knew to reveal that our understanding of the disorder is indeed long overdue.

While the first case of bipolar depression or mania can not be traced, much is known for its development and subsequent classification and names as manic depression — now generally known as bipolar — and of those experts whose breakthroughs have so greatly contributed to our contemporary therapy.

In The Beginning

The early history of bipolar and other mental disorders is, as one would expect, not beautiful, but rather testifies to ignorance, misunderstanding, and fear. In 300-500 AD, according to Cara Gardenswartz, Ph.D., in private practice in Beverly Hills, California, some people with bipolar disorder have had euthanized with specialized knowledge of bipolar disorder and their history.

"These people were seen as" crazy, "possessed by the devil or demons in the earliest documents," says Dr. Gardenswartz. She explained that their treatment or punishment involved restraint or chaining; blood was released; different potions were given, or electrodes were applied to the skull— "many of the ways the sorcerers were treated in different cultures. Indeed, healing has often been used to try and heal, "said Gardenswartz. "We are not familiar with any of the bipolar disorder from 1000 to 1700 AD, but we took a healthier approach to mental disorders in the 18th and 19th centuries." Consider these evolutions of bipolar disorder which the physicist Aretaeus of Cappadocia, an ancient Turkish city, observed and studied in the second century Aretaeus described mania and depression in his academic work on Etiology and Symptomatology of Chronic Illnesses; he believed that they share a common connection and two manifestations of the same illness. The ancient Greeks and the Romans invented the words "crazy" and "melancholia" and used waters in northern Italian spas to handle anxious or euphoric patients, assuming that lithium salts were consumed as a normal resource in a projection of what would happen to them. In 300–400 BC, the ancient Greek philosopher Aristoteles thanked the creative minds of his time for "melancholia." Conversely, people affected by mental illness were considered to be guilty of wrongdoing in the Middle Ages: the illness was certainly an expression of bad deeds, it was considered.

Robert Burton–English scholar, writer, and clergyman–wrote in 1621 a review of 2,000 years of medical and philosophical "wisdom," which many consider being a classic of his time: the Anatomy of Melancholy. This treatise on depression defined him as a mental illness of its own accord. In 1686, ThéophileBonet, a Swiss physician named "manic-melancholic," and linked mania and melancholy.

In the early 1850s, significant progress was made by the diagnosis of foliecirculaire or spiral hysteria by French physician Jean-Pierre Falret–psychotic and suicidal symptoms divided by non-symptom periods. When he described distinct differences between simple depression and increased moods, he broke considerable new academic ground. Throughout 1875, the word "manic-depressive syndrome," a psychiatric disorder, was invented because of his research. Scientists often accept the genetic link correlated with Falret.

"We owe Falret the categorization of bipolar disorder as a disease,' writes in their September 2000 book entitled' Historical Perspectives and the Natural History of Bipolar Disorder,' Jules Angst MD and Robert Sellaro, BSc from Zurich University Hospital, Switzerland.

"It is interesting how Falret's definition of signs and genetic causes matched such a summary in recent books and journals," writes in her 1992 book The Bipolian Syndrome, Manic Depressive Condition, Erika Bukkfalvi Hilliard of Royal Colombian Hospital, in New West-minster, England, MSW, RSW. "Dr. Angst and Sellaro also note that French neurologist and psychiatrist Gabriel François Baillarger used the term folie à double forme to describe cyclic (manic–Depressive) episodes in 1854 and, therefore, the term" folie à double forme "(folie à double forme) is used by the French neurologist Jules Gabriel Baillargeon. Apparently, Baillarger recognized a distinct difference between what we now call bipolar and schizophrenia.

In their treatise, the Swiss specialists detailed in greater detail the face of an emerging disease, especially as regards the' mixed states.' They write:' The story of the concept of mixed states (symptoms of mania and depression at the same time)... was probably already known at the beginning of the 19th century and named' mixtures'... and' middle forms.' The term "mixed states' to J' is also used by Haugsten," Historical aspects of Bipolar disorders in French psychiatry. The son of P. Falret, Jules Falret.

In October 2004 the research paper José Alberto del Porto, Paulista School of Medicine of the University of São Paulo, said: "In the late 19th century, despite contributions by Falret, Baillargeon, and[German psychiatrist Karl Ludwig] Kahlbaum (among others), most of the clinicians still viewed mania and melancholy as distinct and chronically deteriorating entities" The acceptance of this theory would nevertheless not prevail.

Bipolar On Its Own

One of the most recognizable names in the history of bipolar is German psychiatrist Emil Kraepelin (1856–1926). He is sometimes called the founder of contemporary science psychiatry and psychopharmacology. He thought the mental disease had a biological origin. Instead of simply showing the major symptoms, he grouped diseases based on the classification of common patterns of symptoms. This forward-thinking specialist postulated that each major psychiatric disorder was based on a specific brain or other biological pathology. Kraepelin felt that the classification system needed to be revised.

Following extensive research in the early 1900s, EugèneBleuler (1857–1940) coined separate terms "manic-depression" and "dementia praecox," later called schizophrenia. The term "manic depression" was widely utilized until the beginning of the 1930s— even until the 1980s and 1990s. Sigmund Freud, too, broke new ground in the early 1900s when he used psychoanalysis on his manic-depressive patients. In bipolar disorder, it involved childhood trauma and unresolved developmental conflicts.

At the beginning of the 50s, German psychiatrist Karl Leonhard and colleagues started a classification scheme, which led to the term "bipolar." Dr.Gardenswartz notes,' once there was a difference between the bipolar and other disorders, people living with mental illness had been better understood and in turn–together with the advancements of psychopharmacology–received better treatment.' According to prominent psychiatrist Robert L. Spitzer (MD), the term ' bipolar' logically emphasizes' the two poles' of mood-episodes. People with unipolar depression experience episodes with low moods only, while those with bipolar depression experience cyclical depressed and high moods. Dr. Spitzer headed the task force that wrote the 3rd version— unmistakably a significant revision — of the Diagnose and Statistical Manual of Mental Disorders (DSM) of the American Psychological Association (APA). After the 1980 release of DSM-III, the reference work became so influential that the bibie of American psychiatry is often called. (Specialists in many other countries use the ICD) Among the monumental changes to DSM-III, the term "manic-depression" has been dropped, and "bipolar disorder" has been introduced, eliminating patient references as "maniacs." Further revisions of the DSM over the years have clarified inconsistencies in diagnostic criteria and have included references to patients The latest edition, DSM-5, was released by the APA in 2013.

Thomas Insel, MD, former director of the National Institute of Mental Health, a noted American neuroscientist and Psychiatrist, has said that whatever changes to the DSM over the years, the reference work ensures that clinicians use the same terms.

Every version has illustrated developments in psychological theory. For example, the United States The administration of substance abuse and mental health services (SAMHSA) noted that DSM-5 takes an' lifespan ' perspective that acknowledges the importance of age and development when psychiatric disorders start, manifest, and treat.

The DSM-5 release predicted that some of the changes should address the "unrecognition" of bipolar disorders in the International Journal of Bipolar Disorders. The segment "mood disturbances" was historically divided into separate categories for unipolar depressive disorders and bipolar disorders. Apart from bipolar I ("classic" manic depression) bipolar II (depression plus hypomania) and cyclothymic disorder (mood episodes that do not fulfill the full diagnostic criteria for either bipolar I or II), the new chapter also covers a flexible category for "bipolar-like phenomena." The editorial writers felt that in the absence of a current hypo / manic episode, it would make it easier to distinguish bipolar depression and unipolar depression as significant energy and activity upticks would be easier for people to identify and remember in self-reports.

The range of treatments for those with bipolar disorder also evolved and changed with the labeling of psychiatric disorders, says Dr.Gardenswartz. It points to the use of sedatives and barbiturates before the 1950s and to the institutionalization of patients to separate them from others. Several more progressive treatment options arose as prefrontal lobotomies and early types of electroconvulsive shock therapy.

"Beginning in the mid-1900s with the advent of psychiatric and antipsychotic mood-stabilizing medicines, patients were more seen as ill-treated human beings," Dr. Gardenswartz says. Throughout fact, physicians and the media tended to perceive various diseases as "separate entities that they were: autism, constant without breaks or relaxation of symptoms when not treated, or psychotic in which the patients might normally work during the times between this cyclic illness." Lithium has since remained one of the most efficient drugs for bipolar disorders, providing a springboard for further research and discovery. As the ancient Greeks and Romans suspected, natural lithium is indeed found in thermal springs, and their historical use for treating bipolar disorder is scientifically justified.

MogensSchou, MD (1918–2005), Inspired by Dr. Cade, Professor Med. Sci. continued groundbreaking lithium research. Dr. Schou became Professor Emeritus of the Risskov Psychiatric Hospital in Denmark and Honorary Chairman of the International Society for Bipolar Disease. Dr.Schou called his country's manic-depression "the national disease," and Dr.Schou experimentally used lithium in a group of patients who experienced mania in the 1960s. Schou's work showed that lithium could be very effective in treating bipolar mood episodes when properly monitored. Not least due to the efforts of Dr. Schou, the U.S. Food and Drug Administration (FDA) approved lithium for mania as therapeutic therapy in 1970 and 1974 for manic-depressive disorders.

Treatment Triad

In 2020, the treatment of bipolar disorder evolved to recognize the importance of the three pillars of well-being: psychotherapy-supported medication and self-treatment.

Recent pharmacotherapy for bipolar disorder has been extended to include mood stabilizers (the type of lithium), antipsychotics, anti-anxiety drugs (particularly new "atypical" formulations), sleep and antidepressants, under some circumstances.

The specific formulations and dosages to be used vary by the response. It often takes multiple studies of various medications to deter the right combination. This common method is sometimes difficult because there are no accurate experimental tests to determine which medication in a given case is effective— though the researchers are working on it.

Additionally, two forms of brain stimulation have been reported as beneficial for treatment-resistant bipolar depression. One is electroconvulsive therapy. Since its famous shock therapy in the 1940s, it has been greatly refined. Controlled electrical currents are passed through the brain in this technology while the individual is sedated. Transcranial magnetic stimulation (TMS) is an alternative therapy which emits electro-magnetic pulses through the scalp.

Still in the experimental stage: vagus nerve stimulation (VNS), which includes two electrodes implanted in the brain and a pulse generator in the abdomen, and the electric stimuli sent by the system in the thoracic chest to the vagus nerve and the deep brain stimulation (DBS).

Talk therapy had also changed greatly since the 1970s when more action-oriented, humanistic approaches, along with traditional Freudian analysis, became firmly established.

Much scientific evidence suggests that bipolar psychotherapy works better than medication alone when used with medication. Much of this research applies to cognitive behavioral therapy or CBT, as this is the most common psychotherapy type. CBT allows people to identify unhelpful attitudes and behavior to introduce more constructive habits. In a study published in a PLOS ONE journal in 2017, 19 randomized controlled trials found CBT effective at decreasing the rate of relapse and improving symptoms, mania severity, and psychosocial functioning. At least 90 minutes of treatment per session wasthe best result for depression or mania, and people with bipolar I had a lower recurrence rate.

The spectrum of treatment methods is still diversified. A CBT variant adds a component of attention to the traditional approach. Dialectic behavior therapy or DBT incorporates cognitive-computational principles, awareness, and interpersonal skills to help people tolerate painful emotions. Interpersonal and social rhythm therapy (IPSRT) specifically developed for bipolar intervention emphasizes the creation of day-to-day routines, stress management, and the tracking of mood and life events.

Certain strategies include narrative counseling (reframing the history to demonstrate your emotional forces), family-oriented therapy (fostering engagement, problem-solving, and education) and social psychoeducation (information and coping plan provided by a professional facilitator). Peer support, an exchange of experiences without professional involvement, has proved to be a powerful tool for certified peer experts, who typically work in conjunction with behavioral health care practitioners.

Perhaps the biggest transformation since the advent of lithium in bipolar disorder was to move into "patient-centered" or "person-centered" treatment–a result of a larger shift in medicine and psychiatry in the last two decades. The creator is a participant in defining priorities, agreeing on approaches, and implementing specific methods that lead to recovery rather than actively adopting the dictations of health professionals.

A strong body of evidence indicates the improvement of regular exercise, a healthy diet, stress relief strategies, and good sleep in bipolar disorder individuals. Many physicians recommend meditation as part of treatment, and multiple studies suggest that relaxation and compassion are helpful in sustaining health. Mood monitoring–an electronic daily journal of emotional changes and trends in behavior–helps to understand oneself, recognize the causes in mood, and enhance control of symptoms.

It is "blatantly evident" that lifestyle modifications, self-care, and self-management strategies make a real difference, according to Erin E. Michalak, Doctor of Psychiatry at the University of British Columbia. "It is now known that many people with bipolar disorder are using lifestyle interventions not only to manage depression but also increase hypomania and mania," she adds.

Michalak founded and leads the Collaborative RESearch Team to study bipolar disorder (CREST.BD) in psychosocial matters; a Vancouver-based research network focuses on self-management strategies and aims to involve people with bipolar in shaping research.

The Digital Age

In many respects, the surge in the Internet, social media and tablets has made it easier for bipolar to control themselves. Bipolar signs and therapies can be detected more quickly. A community of peers can also be found through forums, books, or portals for self-help. A variety of apps will assist with everything from mood-tracking to awareness exercises.

These applications come within the umbrella of mobile health technology or mHealth, which loosely encompasses information and services related to well being accessed through computers, phones, or wearable devices. Teletherapy, for starters, has gained traction. Regular psychotherapy appointments can be hard for persons living where there are not enough providers or providers–or the community is so small that everybody knows your business. The ease, connectivity, and anonymity of this kind of' personal' therapy for teletherapists outweigh the lack of nonverbal signals that are more noticeable in person while speaking.

Dr.Michalak first conducted a two-phase report in April 2019 in the Mental Health Review of Clinical Internet Research, published to recognize emerging health technology as an important way to help adults with bipolar disorders to maintain a healthy lifestyle. She is a fan of digital technology, also referred to as e-intervention. In her view, though, such services should not be substituted for socially face-to-face relations.

Evan H. Goulding, MD, Ph.D., a deputy professor of psychiatrists and behavioral science at the Feinberg School of Medicine in Northwestern Medicine, says interactive interventions that provide patients with real-time input will improve their patient self-handling.

Goulding received an award from the National Health Institutes to research the use of a mobile Northwestern program called LiveWell: A Wireless Treatment for Bipolar Disorder. A group of people with bipolar I already looking after a doctor checked the technique. Participants provided training packages, regular checks with healthcare mentors, and a frequent recording of their behaviors using digital devices.

"People want to help themselves with resources. It is a tool to be incorporated into everyday life beyond meetings[with practitioners], "says Goulding, noting that study teams are working on psychosocial solutions related to LiveWell in North America and overseas.

Goulding accepts, as a physician, innovations which can give important feedback from the patient to the clinician. Behavioral and physiological data collected directly from real life could enhance understanding of and treatment with bipolar disorder, he said.

In the meantime, medical science continues to pursue the development of methods to enhance depressive treatment. Scientists also explore new medicines, anatomy, biology, alternative choices such as hormone and nutraceuticals (foods providing health benefits), and personalized medication in addition to researching e-interventions. Advances in neuroscience and genetics increase knowledge of the brain-based disease, but very little in clinical practice has yet been translated.

"We've got a lot to be thankful for," Gardenswartz says, "and a lot else to come. We will see a growing distinction in signs and diagnosis over the next several decades and probably the ability to prevent and predict the onset of the condition.

WHAT IS BIPOLAR DISORDER

Bipolar disorder is a mental disorder marked by frequent mood changes. Symptoms can include a high mood known as mania. Episodes of depression can also be included. Bipolar disorder is also called depressive or psychotic syndrome.

People with bipolar disorder may have problems handling or maintaining relationships with everyday life at school or at work. No cure is available, but many treatment options can help to manage the symptoms.

Bipolar Disorder Facts

Bipolar disorder is not an uncommon brain disorder. In reality, it has been reported by 2.8 percent of U.S. adults— or about 5 million individuals. When people with a bipolar disorder start to develop symptoms, the average age is 25 years.

Bipolar depression persists for at least two weeks. A high episode (manic) may last several days or weeks. Some people experience mood changes several times a year, while others may only rarely experience them.

Types Of Bipolar Disorder

Three major types of bipolar disorder are present: bipolar I, bipolar II, and cyclothymia.

1. Bipolar I- The appearance of at least one manic episode defines Bipolar I. Hypomanic, or major depressive episodes may occur before and after the manic episode. This type of bipolar disorder equally affects both men and women.

2. Bipolar II-Those with this form of bipolar disorder have a period of at least two weeks with major depression. We also have a hypomanic episode lasting at least four days. It is assumed that this form of bipolar disorder is more common in women.

3. Cyclothymia-Cyclothymic people experience hypomania and depressive periods. Both signs are slower and less severe than bipolar I or bipolar II mania and depression. Most people with this condition experience stable moods only a month or two.

Your doctor will be able to tell you what type of bipolar disorder you have when talking about your diagnosis.

Bipolar Disorder And Depression

There may be two extremes of bipolar disorder: up and down. You have to undergo a phase of mania or hypomania to be infected with bipolar. In this phase of the disorder, people usually feel "up." If you undergo an upward mood change, you can feel highly optimistic and thrilling.

There is a major depressive episode or "off" condition for some people with bipolar disorder. You may feel lethargic, unmotivated, and sad when you are experiencing a "down" mood change. But not all bipolar disorders with this symptom feel "down" enough to be labeled depressed. For example, for some individuals, a regular mood can seem like sadness while their mania is handled as they liked the "rush" induced by the manic episode.

Although bipolar disorder can make you feel depressed, the condition is not the same as depression. Bipolar disorder can cause lows and highs. But depression always causes "down" moods and emotions.

Causes Of Bipolar Disorder

Bipolar disease is a common mental health problem, but for doctors and researchers, it is a bit of a mystery. What causes some people to develop the condition, and not others is not yet clear.

Possible bipolar disorder causes include:

1. Genetics- If your parent or relative has a bipolar disorder, the disease is more likely to develop than other individuals (see below). Nevertheless, it is important to remember that most people with bipolar disorder do not experience it in their family history.

2. Your brain- The configuration of your brain will influence your disease risk. Structural anomalies or brain functions can increase your risk.

3. Environmental factors- Not only can it make you more likely to develop bipolar disorder in your body. External factors can also lead.

The following factors may include:

- ✓ Extreme stress
- ✓ Traumatic experiences
- ✓ Physical illness

Each of these causes may influence bipolar disorder. Nevertheless, the most likely thing is that a combination of factors leads to the disease's progress.

Is Bipolar Disorder Hereditary?

The mother to the child will pass bipolar disorder. For people with the disorder, the study has established a strong genetic link. If you have a parent, the chances of developing the disorder are four or six times better than those without a family history of the disease.

This does not, though, mean that everybody with family members with the condition can inherit it. Furthermore, not all of the bipolar disorder have a history of the condition in the household.

Genetics still appear to play a major role in the incidence of bipolar disorder. If you have a bipolar family member, find out if screening may be a good idea for you.

Bipolar Disorder Diagnosis

I'm infected with either one or more manic episodes or mixed episodes (manic and depressing). It may also include, but may not include a major depressive episode. One or more major depressive episodes and at least one hypomania diagnosis are diagnosed with bipolar II.

To be treated with an outbreak of manicure, you must have signs that last for at least one week. During this time, you have signed nearly all day long. On the other side, major depressive symptoms must last at least two weeks.

Bipolar disorder can be difficult to diagnose because there may be various mood swings. Diagnosis in children and adolescents is even more complicated. Also, this age group varies more in attitude, attitudes, and strength.

Sometimes bipolar disorder becomes worse when left untreated. Episodes may occur more or more often. But you can live a healthy , productive life if you receive treatment for your bipolar disorder. Diagnosis is, therefore, very necessary. See how the diagnosed bipolar disease is.

Bipolar Disorder Symptoms Test

Every test result is not associated with a bipolar disorder. The specialist will use a number of tests and evaluations instead. These could include:

- ✓ **Medical test:** The specialist must conduct a complete physical evaluation. Physicians can also prescribe blood or urine samples to exclude other possible causes.

✓ **Mental health assessment:** Your doctor may refer you to a psychologist or psychiatrist, such as a mental health professional. These physicians diagnose and treat conditions of mental health such as bipolar disorder. We determine your mental health during the appointment to look for signs of bipolar disorder.

✓ **Mood diary:** If a behavior change caused by a mood disorder like bipolar is suspected by your doctor, you may be asked to map your mood. The easiest way to do this is to keep a journal of how long you like and how long you live. Your doctor may also suggest that you record your patterns of sleep and eating.

✓ **A diagnosis criterion:** The Mental Disorder Diagnosis and Statistical Manual (MDS) describes the signs for various mental health disorders. A list can be used by physicians to validate a depressive disorder.

Numerous methods and examinations can be used by the psychiatrist to treat bipolar disorder. Learn further tests to confirm a diagnosis of a bipolar disorder.

Bipolar Disorder Treatment

There are many medications available to help you manage your bipolar disorder. These include medications, encouragement, and changes in lifestyle. Some natural remedies can also be beneficial.

1. Drugs

Effective drugs may include:

- ✓ Mood stabilizers, for example, lithium (Lithobid)
- ✓ The antipsychotics like olanzapine (Zyprexa)
- ✓ Anti-depressants, such as fluoxetine-olanzapine (Symbyax)
- ✓ A benzodiazepine is a form of anti-anxiety medication, such as alprazolam (Xanax), for short-term use.

2. Psychotherapy

Effective therapies for psychotherapy may include:

- ✓ **Cognitive-behavioral therapy:** CHT is a type of speech therapy. You and a psychiatrist explore how bipolar disorder can be handled. They will help you to understand your patterns of thinking. We can also help you develop constructive approaches for coping.

✓ **Psychoeducation:** Is a form of therapy that lets both you and your loved ones recognize the condition. Learning more aboutbipolar disorder will allow you and others to handle it in your life.

✓ **Interpersonal and social pattern therapy:** (IPSRT) works on managing daily habits such as sleep, eating, and exercise. Balancing these routine values will help you manage your condition.

Additional Treatment Alternatives

✓ Additional treatment choices may include:
✓ Electroconvulsive therapy (ECT)
✓ Sleep medications
✓ Acupuncture

Lifestyle Changes

There are also a few easy steps to help manage the bipolar disorder right now:

✓ Keep a routine for eating and sleeping
✓ Learn to recognize mood swings

✓ Ask a friend or relative to support your treatment plans
✓ Talk to a doctor or licensed healthcare provider

Additional changes in lifestyle can also help relieve symptoms of depression caused by bipolar disorder.

Natural Remedies For Bipolar Disorder

Certain natural remedies can help with bipolar disorder. Nevertheless, after talking to your doctor, it is necessary not to use these treatments. Such therapies can conflict with your medications.

The following remedies and vitamins will help stabilize the condition and relieve bipolar disorder symptoms:

✓ **Fish oil:** A 2013 report shows that people who consume a great deal of seafood and fish oil are less vulnerable to having bipolar disorder. You can eat more fish to get the oil naturally, or you can take an OTC supplement.
✓ **The RhodiolaRosea:** This study also shows that this plant can help to relieve mild depression. It can help treat depressive bipolar disorder symptoms.

✓ **S-adenosylmethionine (SAMe):**SAMe is a replacement to an amino acid. The study has shown that major depression and other mood disorders can alleviate symptoms.

Various other nutrients and vitamins can also reduce bipolar disorder symptoms.

Tips For Coping And Support

You're not alone if you or someone you know has bipolar disorder. Bipolar disorder affects approximately 60 million people worldwide.

One of the best things you can do is to educate yourself and yourself. Several resources are available. Of starters, SAMHSA's locator of mental healthcare services offers ZIP referral detail. Additional resources can also be found on the National Institute of Mental Health website.

If you believe you have symptoms of bipolar disorder, arrange a doctor's appointment. If you believe that a friend, relative, or loved one may have bipolar disorder, it is essential to support and understand. Encourage them to see a doctor if they have any symptoms.

Individuals with a troubling experience may have suicidal thoughts. You should always be careful about suicide.

If you believe someone is immediately at risk of self-harm or injury to someone else:

- ✓ For your local emergency number or Call 911.
- ✓ Remain with the citizen before assistance arrives.
- ✓ Disable all guns, knives, narcotics, or other items that could hurt. Remove.
- ✓ Upon hearing, but don't judge, argue, threaten, or shout.

When suicide is thought by you or someone you meet, seek support from a counselor or a suicide prevention hotline.

Bipolar Disorder And Relationships

Honesty is the best policy when it comes to managing a friendship when you deal with bipolar disorder. Bipolar disorder may impact any relationship in your life, particularly a romantic one. It is, therefore, important to be open to your situation.

The time to tell others you have bipolar disorder is right or wrong. As soon as you are ready, be open and honest. Consider sharing these facts to understand the situation with your partner better:

- ✓ When you have been diagnosed
- ✓ What to expect in your phases of depression.
- ✓ What to do in the manic phases
- ✓ How do you treat your moods?
- ✓ How can they help you?

One of the easiest ways to support and effectively establish a relationship is to commit to your care. Therapy helps you reduce symptoms and reduce the severity of your mood changes. You should concentrate more on the interaction with these facets of the condition under supervision.

You can also know how to foster a healthy relationship with your partner. Consult this guide, which offers advice for you and your wife to maintain healthy relationships when coping with bipolar disorder.

Living With Bipolar Disorder

Bipolar disorder is a persistent psychiatric disorder. Which ensures that you're going to live and deal with it throughout your life. This does not imply, though, that you can not live a happy, healthy life.

Therapy can help you control your mood changes and deal with your symptoms. You may want to set up a support team to help you to get the most out of therapy. You may want to consider a therapist and consultant in addition to your primary doctor. These doctors can help you with the symptoms of bipolar disorder, which medication can not help with talking therapy.

You might also want to find a supportive community. Knowing certain people who also deal with this illness will give you a group of people you can count on and ask for help.

To find treatments that work for you needs perseverance. You need to be patient as you learn to manage bipolar disorder and anticipate mood changes. You will find ways to maintain a normal, happy, and healthy life with your care team.

It can also maintain a sense of perspective regarding life while dealing with a bipolar disorder.

MISCONCEPTIONS

Although the stigma around mental health conditions has taken us a long way in recent years, there is still a long way to go, particularly when it comes to understanding certain conditions, such as bipolar properly.

To support us, we spoke about the current psychiatric misunderstandings which need to be overcome with Rethink Mental Illness and BUPA:

1. That all bipolar is the same

Firstly, two forms of predominant psychiatric disorders are present: bipolar I and bipolar II; Rethink states, "all with bipolar disorder will have various symptom rates." The NHS adds that some people may have only a few bipolar episodes in their lives, and others may have more.

Bipolar is "traditionally marked by depressed lows and manic highs," says Rethink. "Type 1 is marked by greater mania and depression, and typically is tougher than type 2."

2. That it's a personality disorder

It's not likeborderline personality disorder or antisocial personality disorder. Alternatively, it is a condition that mainly affects moods.

3. That it just means 'bad mood swings.'

Whilst it can be a mood disorder, it's not only mood swings that we all get, let's be truthful.

"We are all in good and bad moods sometimes, but mood changes often are more serious for individuals with bipolar disorders, which range from joy and elation (known as madness) to sadness and desperation," says Bupa's clinical director Pablo Vandenabeele. Each mood can be several weeks or normal. Like all mental health problems, mood fluctuations should be taken seriously, not over-simplified or just stigmatized as' mood swings.' What is problematic is that people use the word' bipolar' to define a shift in mood, for people used a long time to explain' OCD,' when the disorder is so much more co-determined

Eleanor Segall, a writer who had bipolar I, explained to Cosmopolitan.com / UK why it's incredibly troubling to use the phrase "You're so bipolar": "Bipolar disorder is a mood disorder, but we don't all constantly ups and downs, and we also didn't cycle quickly between the mood."

4. That being really happy is one of the symptoms

Rethink explains that the' manic high' symptom of bipolar is not really happy.

It could contribute to delirious feelings (e.g., feeling invulnerable) and reckless behavior, which places an individual at risk of being threatened. "Vandenabeele notes that the most common misunderstandings about the illness revolve around the manic phase of his / her disorder.

"A lot of people think all bipolar patients have euphoric elevations," he says. "In fact, however, the manic phase can often be expressed as confidence, irritability, or confusion."

5. That you're ill all the time

Just a few months before her fraud, Eleanor endured insanity, where her visions helped her lose touch with reality. She's been well for long periods- a diagnosis does not mean that you've been plunged into a cycle of sickness.

"Many people with bipolar I and bipolar II symptoms will stay well in treatment for long periods, with a strong network of support and therapy strategy," she notes. "Those who do not take medicine and need it may be unwell, but most of the time and in my situation, you can go through severe mental illness for long periods."

6. That all medication comes with bad side effects

Some antidepressant drugs may have side effects, yes. But this is not the case with all medicines, and it is very often the case that a person or a trial and error process finds out which medicines work best for you.

Eleanor says that her anti-psychotic therapy had some side effects, but that ultimately meant that she could get better. Remember to negotiate the right medicine with your doctor or therapist.

7. That it stops you from living a normal life

That, of course, is not true at all. As with any illness, you can lead a great normal life if it is managed, and you have the right medicine and care.

Eleanor is perfect proof that this is not the case, as is, of course, Mariah Carey.

"I still had my A levels, moved to study, and now I'm employed as an independent journalist," says Eleanor. "There's a misunderstanding around the bipolar disorder, which assumes that you won't have the ability to live a regular, fulfilled life. People believe you will never be able to work or get academically, have the family, or have relationships. That assumption is incorrect.

Harmful Bipolar Disorder Myths You Should Stop Believing

What has famous singers including Demi Lovato, Russell Brand, Jane Pauley, the news anchor, and Catherine Zeta-Jones, in common? They live with bipolar disorder, like millions of others. I learned very little about the disease until I got my diagnosis in 2012. In my family, I didn't even know it ran. And I learned, read books after books, listened to my physicians, and educated myself until I understood what was going on.

As we read more about bipolar disorder, several misunderstandings also exist. There are a few misconceptions and evidence here to give you information and to help end the stigma.

1. Myth: A rare condition is a bipolar disorder.

Fact: In the United States alone, bipolar disorder impacts 2 million people. One in five Americans has a condition of mental health.

2. Myth: Bipolar disorder only changes in the attitude that everyone has.

Fact: Bipolar disorder highs and lows are very distinct from normal mood swings. People with bipolar disorder experience extreme changes that are not typical of energy, activity, and sleep.

"When you wake up happily, feel grumpy in the morning, and end up smiling again, it doesn't imply you have a bipolar disorder–no matter how often it occurs for you! The psychological study advisor at a US hospital that wants to stay confidential! Even a diagnosis of fast cycle bipolar disorder requires many days, rather than just hours, in a series of (hypo)manic symptoms. Clinicians look for symptom groups rather than emotions.

3. Myth: Only one kind of bipolar disorder occurs.

Fact: There are four common forms of bipolar disorder, with a different experience per person.

Bipolar I is treated if a patient experiences one or more depressive episodes and one or more manic episodes, sometimes with psychiatric features including paranoia or misunderstandings.

Bipolar II has its main feature depressive episodes and at least one hypomanic episode. Hypomania is a less severe mania. An individual with bipolar II disorder can have depressive symptoms that correspond to depression or incongruous mood.

Multiple cyclothymic symptom cycles, as well as multiple phases of depressed symptoms lasting two or more years (1 year in both children and adolescents) without fulfilling the severe criteria for hypomanic and depressive spells, are classified as cyclothymic disorders.

Otherwise, not mentioned bipolar disorder does not adopt a certain trend and is characterized by signs of bipolar disorder that do not conform to the three above definitions.

4. Myth: Diät and diet will treat bipolar disorder.

Fact: Bipolar disorder is a lifelong disease that does not exist at the moment. Nevertheless, it can be best handled by medications and talk therapy by tension reduction and daily sleep, food, and workout habits.

5. Myth: Mania's widespread. You're well moored, and you're fun to be around.

Fact: A psychotic person can feel good at first in certain cases, but events can be devastating and even frightening without treatment. You can go to a large shopping stream and invest more than your budget. Many may get too stressed or overly irritable, get irritated with little issues, and grab loved ones. A manic person may lose control and even lose touch with reality.

6. Myth: Bipolar performers would lose their talent if they are punished.

Fact: Therapy also helps you to think more clearly, potentially enhancing your job. This was found personally by Pulitzer-nominated novelist MaryaHornbacher.

"I was very convinced that when I was diagnosed with bipolar disorder, I could never write again. Yet I published one book ago, now I'm on my seventh. "She finds that her experience in recovery is even stronger.

"I haven't been treated for bipolar disorder when I was working on my second book, and I wrote about 3,000 pages of the worst book you ever saw. And then, I got diagnosed, and I was handled in the middle of writing the novel I couldn't compete, and I kept writing because of writing. And in 10 months or so, I wrote the book itself, the work that was eventually written. Since I have been diagnosed with my bipolar disorder, I have been able to harness and concentrate on imagination effectively. Now I'm struggling with some signs, but I only go about my day in general, "she added. "It's definitely livable when you get a grip on it. It is treatable. It is treatable. You can work with it. You can. She writes of her struggles in her memoir "Madness: A Bipolar Life," and currently works on a follow-up novel on her path to recovery.

7. Myth: Bipolar disorder is always manic or depressed. Myth:

Fact: People with bipolar disorder have a long, calm, healthy mood known as euthymia. On the other side, they can sometimes undergo what is considered a "mixed-phase," which has both mania and sadness.

8. Myth: Both bipolar disorder drugs are the same.

Fact: It may take a trial and a mistake to find the drug that works for you. "Most cognitive stabilizers / antipsychotic drugs are essential for the diagnosis of bipolar disorder. Something that functions for someone who could not function for someone else. If you try and don't work or have side effects, it is very important that you let your provider know. The provider should be there to work together with the patient in order to find the fit, "the research manager for psychiatry wrote.

SYMPTOMS OF BIPOLAR

For different people, bipolar disorder may look very different. Their form, extent, and frequency vary widely. Many people are more susceptible to mania or sadness, while others vary between the two periods fairly. Some of them have multiple mood disorders, while others only suffer a few in their entire lives.

Within bipolar disorder, there are four different kinds of mood periods: mania, hypomania, agitation, and mixed phases. Every type of episode of bipolar mood has a unique set of symptoms.

Mania Signs

In the manic phase of bipolar disorder, sensations of increased strength, inspiration, and euphoria are typically felt. You can speak one mile a minute, sleep very little, and be hyperactive if you have a manic episode. You might also feel all-powerful, unstoppable, or great-destined.

But while mania at first feels good, it continues to spiral out of control. During a manic episode, you can play away savings, engage in improper sexual activity, or make foolish business investments, for instance. You can also get furious, irritable, and violent, choosing wars, rattle them out if some fail to comply, and blame anyone who criticizes your actions. Some people become delusional or even begin to hear voices.

Common signs and mania symptoms include:

- ✓ Unusually ' strong ' and confident OR very irritable
- ✓ Unrealistic, grandiose expectations in our expertise or strength
- ✓ Sleeping very little, still very energetic
- ✓ Speaking too fast that people can't keep up
- ✓ Take a race; leap from one concept to the next rapidly
- ✓ Highly distractible, unable to focus
- ✓ The judgment and impulsiveness are impaired
- ✓ Perform recklessly without considering the consequences
- ✓ The visions and paranoia (in severe cases)

Symptoms Of Hypomania

Hypomania is a less serious form of mania. You can feel euphoric, optimistic, and efficient in a hypomanic condition, but can proceed with your daily life without losing touch with reality. It may seem to some that you are just in an unusually good mood. Hypomania can, though, lead to bad decisions that destroy the friendship, career, and reputation. Hypomania is often followed up with full-blown mania or a major depressive episode.

Symptoms Of Bipolar

Depression Bipolar depression has, in the past, been associated with regular depression, but a growing body of research suggests there are considerable differences between both, especially when treatment is recommended. Antidepressants are not effective in most patients with bipolar depression. In addition, antidepressants can worsen the bipolar syndrome, contributing to mania or hypomania, rapid cycling between moods, or interfering with other mood-stabilizing medicines.

Notwithstanding several differences, some signs of bipolar depression are more pronounced than in normal depression. During the bipolar depression, for example, irritability, remorse, erratic mood swings, and restlessness is more likely to occur. You will walk and chat gradually, sleep a lot, and gain weight in bipolar depression. Furthermore, you are more likely to develop psychotic depression, a condition in which you lose touch with reality, and have serious work and social problems.

Common bipolar depression symptoms include:

- ✓ Feeling hopeless, sad, or empty
- ✓ Irritability
- ✓ Inability to experience pleasure
- ✓ Fatigue or loss of energy
- ✓ Physical and mental sluggishness
- ✓ Appetite or weight changes
- ✓ Sleep problems
- ✓ Concentration and memory problems
- ✓ Feelings of worthlessness or guilt
- ✓ Thoughts of death or suicide

Symptoms Of A Mixed Episode

A mixed episode of bipolar disorder has both mania or hypomania and depression symptoms. Depression associated with anger, irritability, nausea, insomnia, distractibility, and rapid thinking are common signs of a mixed event. The high-energy and attitude mix poses a particularly high risk of suicide.

What Is Quick Cycling?

Many persons with bipolar disorder experience a "fast cycle," in which four or more mania or depressive periods arise within a 12-month span. Mood swings can happen very quickly, like a rapidly shifting roller coaster over days or even hours from high to low and back again. Fast spinning will bring you out of balance, and most often happens if your symptoms are not properly treated.

Depressive Depression Treatment

Wait for treatment if you see signs of a bipolar disorder in yourself or someone else. Ignoring the problem won't make it go, it's almost certainly going to get worse. Living with untreated bipolar disorder can lead to problems in all aspects of your career to your health. However, bipolar disorder is highly treatable, so the diagnosis of the problem and the start of treatment can help prevent such complications as soon as possible.

If you are unwilling to seek help because you like how you look, note the vitality and euphoria come at a cost. Mania and hypomania often make you and the people around you destructive.

Basic Treatment

✓ **Bipolar disorder requires long-term care-** Since a persistent, recurrent condition is bipolar disorder, continued treatment is necessary even if you feel better. Many people with bipolar disorder require medication to avoid and maintain symptoms clear of new episodes.

✓ **There is more to recovery than medication-** Medication alone is typically not enough to fully control the effects of bipolar disorder. The most successful depressive treatment approach requires a mixture of medicine, counseling, lifestyle changes, and social support.

Self Help For Bipolar Disorder

It is not always easy to cope with bipolar disorder. But to manage bipolar disorder successfully, you have to make smart choices. Your diet and daily habits will greatly influence your moods and even reduce your drug needs.

Symptoms In Children And Adolescents

Symptoms with bipolar disorder can be difficult to identify in children and adolescents. It is often difficult to know if these are natural ups and downs, the effects of depression or loss, or symptoms of a non-bipolar mental health problem.

Children and adolescents might have severe suicidal, psychotic, or hypomanic episodes, but the history of the disorder may differ from that of depressed adults. And moods will change quickly during episodes. Many children may have intervals in events without mood signs.

For children and adolescents, the most common symptoms of bipolar disorder may include extreme mood changes that vary from normal mood changes.

The Keys To Bipolar Disorder Self-Help

✓ **Get educated-** Know as much about bipolar disorder as you can. Get informed. The more you know, the better you will help your own recovery.
✓ **The move-** Training has an advantageous effect on mood and can reduce the number of bipolar episodes. Aerobic exercise that stimulates the activity of the arm and leg, such as running, jumping, surfing, spinning, ascending, and drumming, will particularly help the brain and nervous system.

- ✓ **Maintain stress in control–** Avoid situations of high stress, maintain a healthy work and life balance, and try relaxation techniques like meditation, yoga, or profound breathing.
- ✓ **Seek support-** It's important to have people you can turn to for help and motivation. Try joining or connecting to a trusted friend in a support group. Reaching out is not a sign of weakness, and it does not indicate for others that you are a burden. In reality, most friends will be flattered to trust them fully, and only friendship will be improved.
- ✓ **Take care of friends and family-** Nothing is so soothing to your nervous system as face-to-face interaction with loving people who can listen to you speak about what you feel.
- ✓ **Make healthy choices-** Sleeping and exercising will help stabilize your moods. Healthy choices. It is especially important to maintain a regular sleep schedule.
- ✓ **Track your moods-** Keep track of your symptoms and watch for signs that your moods are spinning out of balance so that you can stop the problem before it begins.

Bipolar Depression And Suicide

Often a very severe depressive period in bipolar disorder and suicide is a significant risk factor. Yes, people with bipolar disorder are more prone to suicide than people with regular depression. In fact, their efforts at suicide appear to be more deadly.

For individuals with bipolar disorder with repeated depressant symptoms, mixed spells, drug or drogue use, a family history of suicide, or early onsets, the risk of suicide is even greater.

The warning signs of suicide include:

- ✓ Talking about death, self-harm, or suicide
- ✓ Feeling hopeless or helpless
- ✓ Feeling worthless or like a burden to others
- ✓ Acting recklessly, as if one has a "death wish."
- ✓ Putting affairs in order or saying goodbye
- ✓ Seeking out weapons or pills that could be used to commit suicide

Causes And Triggers

There is no single cause ofbipolar disorder. Many people appear to be predisposed genetically tobipolar syndrome, but not everyone with hereditary susceptibility experiences the condition, which means that the genes are not the only source. Many brain imaging studies show that people with bipolar disorders have physical changes in their brains. Other research points to neurotransmitter imbalances, thyroid abnormality, circadian rhythmic disruptions, and high-stress hormone levels of cortisol.

Furthermore, the development ofbipolar disorder is thought to involve external environmental and psychological factors. These outside causes are referred to as stimuli. Triggers can trigger new manic or depressed episodes or aggravate existing symptoms. However, many episodes of bipolar disorder happen without an apparent trigger.

- ✓ **Stress–** Depressive bipolar disorder in someone with hereditary susceptibility may cause stressful life events. Such incidents also include abrupt or unexpected shifts, good or bad, such as engagement, a college split, loss of a loved one, explosion, or gestures.
- ✓ **Substance Abuse–** While substance abuse does not cause bipolar disorder, it can contribute to illness and exacerbate the path of the disease. Drugs like cocaine, ecstasy, and amphetamines can trigger mania and trigger depression by alcohol and tranquilizer.

- ✓ **The pramice–** Some medicines, especially antidepressant medicines, can trigger mania. Other medicines that can induce mania include cold medicine on the market, suppressants of appetite, nicotine, corticosteroids, and thyroid medications.
- ✓ **Seasonal Changes–** Anxiety and stress symptoms also adopt seasonal trends. Manic episodes are more frequent in summer and depressive episodes in autumn, winter and spring are more severe.
- ✓ **Sleep Deprivation–** Sleep loss, sometimes as little as a few hours of rest, may cause an episode of mania.

When To See A Doctor

With intense moods, people with bipolar disorder often don't know how much emotional instability disturbs their families and relationships and don't receive the treatment they deserve.

And if you are like people with bipolar disorder, you can have a more successful euphoria so periods. This euphoria, though, is always accompanied by an emotional collapse that could leave you sad, worn-out, and even political, legal, or relationship problems.

See your psychiatrist or mental health provider if you have any symptoms of depression or mania. Bipolar disorder is not improving on its own. Getting treatment from a mental health professional with bipolar disorder expertise will help control the symptoms.

When To Get Emergency Help

Suicide thoughts and actions are popular in people with bipolar disorder. If you are concerned, dial 911 or your local emergency phone, go to an emergency room, or support a family member or friend.

If you have a loved one who is atthe risk of suicide or who attempted suicide, make sure that someone sticks with him. Immediately call 911 or the local emergency line. And take the person to the closest emergency hospital if you believe that you can do it safely.

CAUSES OF BIPOLAR

The cause ofbipolar disorder is not fully understood. Genetic, neurochemical, and environmental factors undoubtedly combine to play a role in the development and persistence of bipolar disorder on many different levels. Apparently, it is a neurobiological condition, which happens in a certain part of the brain and is triggered by a deficiency of certain brain chemicals (which both exist in the brain and body). Three specific brain chemicals — Gaba, dopamine, and noradrenaline have been implicated. It can lie unconscious and be automatically stimulated as a neurobiological condition or can be caused by stressors of life.

Although no one understands exactly what causes bipolar disorder, some significant hints have been discovered by researchers:

Genetic factors in bipolar disorder

Since bipolar disorder seems to be common in cultures, certain genetic factors appear to be at least at risk. Approximately half of the people withthe bipolar syndrome have a mood disorder family member such as depression.

If one parent has a bipolar disorder, his or her child is 10 to 15 percent more likely to develop this condition. The frequency in an infant rises to 30-40% if both parents have a bipolar disorder.

Studies carried out on identical twins reveal that if one twin is diagnosed with bipolar disorder, the likelihood of the other twin often rises from 40 to 70 percent.

Studies of adopted twins (where a child whose biological parent has been ill and raised untouched by the illness in an adoptive family) have helped researchers learn more about genetic causes versus causes of ecological and life events.

Although all this evidence is interesting, it is not definitive about the neurological origins of bipolar disorder. Further research is needed to understand better the genetic factors involved.

Neurochemical factors in bipolar disorder

Bipolar disorder is primarily a biological disorder in a particular brain area that is caused by the dysfunction of certain neurotransmitters or chemical messengers in the brain. Neurotransmitters such as norepinephrine, serotonin, and potentially many others may be included in these compounds. It can be inactive and disabled alone as a biochemical condition, or it can be caused by external factors such as psychological stress or social circumstances.

Environmental factors in bipolar disorder

- ✓ A life event can trigger a bipolar mood episode in a person with a genetic condition.
- ✓ The event may occur even without specific genetic factors, altering health habits, drug or alcohol usage, or hormonal problems.
- ✓ Bipolar disorder among people at risk of disease appears at an increasingly early age. A significant rise in previous events may be attributed to a prior under-diagnosis of the condition. This change in the age of onset could be caused by unintelligible social and environmental factors.
- ✓ While drug abuse is not known as a cause of the bipolar disorder, it may exacerbate the condition by interfering with recuperation. Alcohol, drugs, or tranquilizers can lead to a more severe phase of depression.

What is medication-triggered mania?

In people vulnerable to bipolar disorder, medications such as antidepressants can trigger a manic episode. Therefore, in those with manic episodes, a depressive event must be handled carefully. Because a depressive episode can become a psychotic episode when opioid treatment is administered, it is also advised that an anti-manic medicine should avoid an episode of manicure. Anti-manic medicine creates a "ceiling" that partially protects the person against antidepressant mania.

Some other drugs can cause a "rush" like mania. For starters, appetite suppressants may cause increased energy, lower sleep, and more talkative behavior. Nonetheless, after the medication ends, the individual returns to his usual mood.

Substances which may contribute to a manic episode include:

✓ Illicit drugs like cocaine and "developing products" like methamphetamine and amphetamines.
✓ Excessive doses, including appetite suppressants and cold preparations of certain over-the-counter medicinal products

- ✓ Nonpsychiatric drugs, such as Thyroid medicines and corticosteroids, such as prednisone.
- ✓ Excessive caffeine (moderate levels of caffeine are fine).

If an individual is prone to bipolar disorder, tension, regular use of stimulants or alcohol, and lack of sleep, the condition can start quickly. Many medications may also cause a suicidal or psychotic phase. If you have a family history of bipolar disorder, alert the health care provider to avoid the risk of a manic episode triggered by drugs.

EFFECT OF BIPOLAR

Bipolar disorder is a brain-based condition, previously referred to as manic depression. The disorder is distinguished by one or several periods of psychotic or "mixed" spells and may include a major depressive episode in some instances. While depression is usually associated with the condition, we also recognize that a bipolar syndrome does not include, though it does, depressive episodes. However, the condition will influence nearly any other part of your body, from your energy levels to your muscle appetite and even libido.

Throughout cycles with manic episodes, bipolar disorder is described.

You have above-average energy levels during a manic phase and can not sleep well. You can also be irritated, restless, and enhanced by sex. This step can have the same effects on the body if you develop depression. You can feel a sudden energy shortage and need more sleep, and feel depressed and hopeless. Changes in appetite can also occur if the individual develops depression. Depression, like mania, can also induce irritability and restlessness.

A combined state between mania and depression can also be felt. In both stages, you can find signs.

Central Nervous System

Bipolar disorder mainly affects the central nervous system's brain.

The central nervous system is composed of both the brain and the spine, consisting of a series of nerves that control various activities of the body.

Some of the results are:

- ✓ Irritability
- ✓ Aggressiveness
- ✓ Hopelessness
- ✓ Feelings of guilt
- ✓ Severe sadness
- ✓ Loss of interest in activities you normally enjoy
- ✓ Being in an excessively good mood
- ✓ Overactivity
- ✓ Feelings of hyperactivity
- ✓ Being easily distracted
- ✓ Forgetfulness
- ✓ Being overly defensive
- ✓ Having a provocative attitude

Bipolar disorder can also make focusing challenging. You could notice your mind racing in the midst of a manic phase and have trouble controlling your thoughts. You will talk much faster than usual. A stressful episode also can cause problems with focus, but the mind can feel much slower than normal. You can feel anxious and find it difficult to make decisions. Your recall can be weak, too.

Bipolar disorder may impact your sleeping and dropping capacity. Manic periods sometimes indicate that you have very little sleep, and depressive episodes may contribute to more or less sleep than average. In both instances, it is not uncommon to have insomnia.

For bipolar disorder, insomnia can be especially dangerous because you might be more tempted to take sleeping pills. Both effects are related more to mania than to depression.

Cardiovascular System

With comparison to bipolar disorder, if you have insomnia, it can also impact the cardiovascular system.

Including:

- ✓ Heart palpitations
- ✓ Rapid heart rate
- ✓ An increased pulse

The higher heartbeat may also be higher than normal blood pressure.

The National Institute for Mental Health (NAMI) states people with bipolar disorder are at higher risk of being hospitalized with agitation or treatment avoidance hyperactivity disorder (ADHD).

Endocrine System

Your endocrine system includes hormones that rely heavily on brain messages. If these signals are interrupted, hormone variations can occur.

Bipolar disorder can induce libido changes. Mania can overload your sex drive, while depression can significantly reduce it. Some people are misjudged with this disorder, which can also increase the risk of poor sexual health decisions. Bipolar disorder can also influence your weight, especially during the depression. You might experience a decrease in appetite with depression, resulting in weight loss. It is also possible to experience the reverse of your hunger, which could raise your weight.

Skeletal And Muscular Systems

Bipolar disorder doesn't directly affect bones and the body, but it can affect the nervous and muscular processes if you suffer from depressive episodes. Depression can lead to unexplained pains and aches that can make it hard to manage everyday activities. It may also be difficult to exercise because of your discomfort. Throughout fact, whether you suffer stress, exhaustion and discomfort are normal and may be caused by too much sleep or an inability to sleep.

Gastrointestinal System

Bipolar anxiety can make feeling tired and irritable. It can impact your immune system as well.

Some of the following results include:

- ✓ Abdominal pain
- ✓ Diarrhea
- ✓ Nausea
- ✓ Vomiting

These symptoms often involve feelings of panic or imminent doom. You could also sweat and breathe quickly

Other Effects

Bipolar disorder may impact the job or school results. It can also find establishing and maintaining relationships challenging.

Additional effects may include:

- ✓ Heavy alcohol use
- ✓ Drug misuse
- ✓ Spending sprees
- ✓ Unrealistic beliefs in your own abilities

Most people with bipolar disorder are still actively working people and can live a healthy professional and personal life. Untreated bipolar disorder can exacerbate your daily life and interfere.

In both psychotic and depressed periods, suicidal thoughts and actions can occur.

Effects On The Family

Bipolar disorder is a brain disorder with extreme mood changes. It is a disease that affects not only the patient but also their family and friends. Living with a person with bipolar disorder requires learning how to cope with symptoms ' difficulties, support the ill person, and find effective ways to cope.

The family can be affected in a number of ways depending on the nature of an individual's disease and on how well the disease is handled. If mood changes are moderate, the family can recover from some anxiety, but they can learn how to live with the needs of the condition over time and with knowledge around mental illness. Care of someone with more severe symptoms can be very stressful for the family, especially if the skills needed to cope with mental illness are not developed. It can be tiring, especially for families with small children.

In the following ways, bipolar disorder can affect families:

- ✓ Emotional distress such as guilt, grief, and worry
- ✓ Disruption in regular routines
- ✓ Having to deal with unusual or dangerous behavior
- ✓ Financial stresses as a result of a reduced income or excessive spending
- ✓ Strained marital or family relationships
- ✓ Changes in family roles
- ✓ Difficulty in maintaining relationships outside the family
- ✓ Health problems as a result of stress

Family members will feel a wide range of emotions as they learn to deal with someone with bipolar disorder. There is no correct or incorrect way to feel. Whether you treat these emotions is significant.

Like every serious disease, communities would probably feel pain and sadness. This is a natural response. We love and want our communities to be healthy and happy. Families feel that they have often forgotten the person they learned. Nevertheless, a mental illness such as bipolar disorder does not mean a healthy, pleasant existence can not be lived. What it means is that people and their communities face a new obstacle.

Families are also worried about their loved one because a manic episode will lead an individual to act riskily and dangerously. One way of helping to reduce this concern is to create a plan to manage the family in difficult times. If the family member feels good, sit down and talk about how things are done in case they become uncomfortable. A crisis plan can help ensure that everyone knows what to expect and what to do if they are reluctant again.

Children may be afraid of inheriting the disease. Older children may be afraid of managing the care of their ill siblings when their parents can't do the job anymore. In any case, families will benefit from learning to manage these concerns so that they do not have a happy and fulfilling way of life.

What Families Can Do

- ✓ Educate yourself on the epidemic
- ✓ Help your family member to control the condition
- ✓ To believe in them, especially in times when they can't trust themselves
- ✓ Continue to love them, even if you give up

"I still think about what could happen while my wife is in a manic state. I will handle so long as I know that she will change. I can't give up hope." Education and support won help families with a bipolar disorder family immensely.

BIPOLAR DISORDER VS DRUG ADDICTION

Previously defined as manic depression, bipolar disorder is a severe mental disorder marked by frequent and violent attitudes, actions, and energy adjustments.

Including drug abuse, bipolar disorder poses a risk to the physical and emotional well-being of people. Bipolar disorder sufferers are higher than their general population in terms of relationship problems, economic instability, accidental injuries, and suicides. We are also much more likely to develop a drug or alcohol problem.

Statistics from the American Journal of Managed Care shows:

- ✓ About 56 percent of people with bipolar who enrolled in a national study had a lifelong addiction to drugs or alcohol.
- ✓ About 46 percent of that population had exploited or had been drug dependent.
- ✓ About 41 percent had drug abuse or were drug-addicted.
- ✓ The alcohol is the most frequently abused substance in bipolar.

If you have a bipolar disorder and drug or alcohol addiction, you may have a concurrent diagnosis of bipolar disorder and drug abuse. Dual diagnosis or a co-occurring condition may cause recuperation more complicated. Bipolar persons will experience intense agitation combined with increased activity and excessive self-importance periods. Such emotional instability will conflict with your therapy program and make it difficult to follow the care plan instructions.

Dual assessment treatment programs are designed to respond to the needs of people experiencing this dynamic psychiatric condition. With specially trained and accredited mental health professionals and addiction specialists, these centers offer treatments that integrate the best bipolar treatment strategies with the most effective addictive treatments.

How Are Bipolar And Addiction Related?

The high rate of substance abuse and chemical dependency in bipolar persons is not easily explained. One reason is that a high percentage of people try to self-medicate drugs and alcohol in order to numb the painful symptoms of their bipolar disorder.

Symptoms of bipolar disorder such as fear, pain, fatigue, and sleeplessness are so disturbing that many people are turning to drugs and alcohol for a little longer to relieve distress. On the other side, the National Institute of Mental Health states that drinking and using drugs in someone with bipolar disorder can cause depressive or psychotic moods.

Age and sex will play a role in the bipolar-addiction partnership. Substance abuse is more common in young people than in other population groups, according to the Bipolar Disorder report. Young men take dangerous chances or behave on serious self-destructive impulses more than women or older men. The incidence of substance abuse is much lower for elderly people with bipolar disorder.

Clinical scientists believe brain chemistry can influence both bipolar disorder and the misuse of drugs. People with bipolar disorder often have an elevated amount of WebMD-based serotonin, dopamine, and norepinephrine. These chemicals affect vital functions such as appetite, metabolism, sleep, and the response of your body to stress. We control attitude and feelings as well.

Regular use of drugs or alcohol that interfere with the control of these chemicals in your brain, causing an emotional disturbance, excessive energy, and depression.

People with bipolar disorder can use drugs or alcohol because they are not aware of the need to stabilize their moods. Substance abuse often has the opposite effect, increasing the effects of bipolar disorder.

Symptoms Of Bipolar Disorder

We all experience intense episodes of sadness, anger, or despair. But these symptoms are all-consuming and uncontrollable for someone who fits the diagnostic criteria for bipolar disorder. There are four main types of mood episodes, which characterize bipolar disorder: mania, hypomania, depression, and mixed episodes.

- ✓ Mania
- ✓ Hypomania
- ✓ Depression
- ✓ Mixed Episodes

Treatment For Bipolar And Addiction

Bipolar disorder and opioid dependence had historically been presented as distinct disorders and handled in different facilities. People with a diagnosis of bipolar disorder were referred to mental health care centers or psychiatric hospitals, while drug and alcohol abusers were rehabilitated.

Addiction practitioners now recognize the importance of concurrently addressing bipolar disorder and drug abuse via a process called "comprehensive therapy." Comprehensive care includes various recovery approaches. Your treatment plan may include one-on-one mental health psychotherapy, addiction specialist counseling, dual diagnosis groups, family counseling, and holistic therapy.

Features of the bipolar disorder and addiction integrated program include:

✓ Centralized treatment in one rehabilitation facility
✓ A joint network of psychiatrists, alcohol specialists and other practitioners specialized in double-diagnosis care
✓ Personal psychotherapy, which is intended to control the feelings and reduce the risk of drug abuse
✓ A psychological medication to help you cope with bipolar disorder ups and downs
✓ Support of the peer group from others who fight addiction and mood disorder

It is not sufficient to treat bipolar disorder without tackling the substance abuse problem and vice versa. If you are not vigilant for both factors, the odds of recurrence are high. Relapse avoidance approaches should include coping skills for the control of psychological and mental causes of substance abuse in a person with bipolar disorder.

How Does Drug Abuse Affect Someone With Bipolar Disorder?

Bipolar disorder is an extreme mood disorder marked by irregular behavior, behavior, and energy levels associated with everyday life.

It has been estimated that 2.8 percent of the American adult population suffered from bipolar disorder over the last year, based on 2001-2003 reports, according to the National Institute of Mental Health (NIMH).

An individual must have had at least one manic episode to be diagnosed with bipolar I disorder. An individual must have at least one hypomanic episode, and at least one major depressive episode in order to be diagnosed with bipolar II disorder and not had any manic episodes

Mania involves an expansive, high, or irritable mood and enhanced energy or activity. Both have to be rare and constant. It must take place during a different period lasting at least one week and must be available nearly every day for the greater part of the day. Madness may also be treated with short episodes if they are too serious about being admitted. If hospitalization is not necessary, the episode must also impede or involve psychosis significantly. There must also be a number of specific symptoms in the show to be classified with mania. Finally, medications or any other medical condition or action should not be blamed for the incident.

Hypomania is close to mania, but must only be treated for 4 days. It can not require hospitalization, impair operation greatly, or cause hysteria. The episode must be a clear change in functioning, and it must be realistic for others to detect this improvement in functioning and attitude.

A significant episode of depression includes a depressed mood and/or lack of enjoyment or desire. There must be a series of specific symptoms for a duration of 2 weeks. The role must shift, and the event may cause significant suffering or serious injury. The incident must not be triggered by medicine or any other medical condition and must not be a suitable response to a substantial loss.

Alcohol and drugs can appear to be a good way to alleviate the effects of bipolar disorder and can be used as a method for self-medication to treat symptoms. Of starters, weed or alcohol may be used to alleviate irritability in a manic episode. An individual may use a stimulant, such as cocaine or methamphetamine, during a depressed episode to try to boost their energy. Although it may seem like using this or other substances in the short term, it is a dangerous way of dealing with them as they can do more harm than good. To add to the inherent danger of violence, substance abuse will intensify and make it more difficult to handle bipolar disorder.

Bipolar Disorder, Drugs, And The Brain

Several elements can help bipolar disorder develop. Genetic factors play a part, and some specific genes have even been identified by researchers. Biochemical considerations are also known to be concerned. Changes in the structures of norepinephrine, epinephrine, and serotonin can lead to mania and depression. The degree of glutamate may also be linked with bipolar disorder. Research also shows that disruption of the control of calcium within cells may lead to mania. Furthermore, hormone imbalances and hypothalamic-hypophysial-adrenal axis symptoms, which include stress reaction, may also be causes of bipolar disorders.

Neurophysiological influences can also lead. Bipolar disorder is an emotional network, as well as increased activation of regions that affect the experience of emotions and the development of emotional response, has been associated with reduced activation and decreased gray matter.

Drugs and alcohol also interfere with the physiology of the brain and influence other brain regions. Some can stimulate nerve cells because they are identical to normal (chemical) neurotransmitters. Others can induce cells to release too many neurotransmitters or to inhibit cells from recycling neurotransmitters as they should. All these results will affect natural nerve cell contact.

✓ Certain medications stimulate the brain reward circuit unnecessarily, causing the user to use the medication regularly. Therefore, an anxiety and irritability circuit of the brain may improve vulnerability, as opioid consumption grows. When the consumption of drugs occurs daily, nerve cells become used to substance use and usually still function on narcotics, a phenomenon known as dependency. Withdrawal symptoms can worsen if the person stops using the drug. Drug use may also affect the pre-frontal cortex, which plays a role in the ability of a person to think, solve problems, make decisions, plan, and control impulses. Many drugs often impact many brain areas, such as the brain stem.

✓ Since both the use of medications and bipolar disorder are related to brain changes, medication can have a larger impact as mental health illness is combated. Research shows that adults who have bipolar disorder and drug use disorder have more irregular activity in the brain, the fewer amount of gray matter, and more deficiencies in the brain neurotransmitter network than adults who have bipolar syndrome but have no co-occurring impairment of substance usage.

Brain changes may also describe or partly explain why these conditions frequently overlap with one another. One study suggests that the impact of depression on an activated brain (Orbitofrontal Cortex) in individuals who use drugs before their bipolar disorder progresses may contribute to quicker development of mania. In fact, bipolar disorder can be correlated with orbitofrontal cortex defects, and these deficits may increase the tendency to take drugs in those who initially experience bipolar disorder.

Complications Of Co-Occurring Bipolar Disorder And Addiction

People with bipolar disorder often use drugs or alcohol. A study in Current Psychiatry journal states that nearly 60 percent of those who have been diagnosed with bipolar I disorder have sometimes had a condition of the use of a drug. When multiple disorders, like the use of a substance and a bipolar disorder, happen in the same person, they are called co-occurring disorders. Problems associated with the co-occurring disease with drug use and bipolar disorder may include:

- ✓ The outcome of early depression problems
- ✓ Poorer result
- ✓ More suicide trials
- ✓ Higher rate of anxiety disorders
- ✓ Higher numbers of distressed periods
- ✓ More regular hospitalizations
- ✓ Higher rates of injuries
- ✓ A higher level of heavy riding
- ✓ Poorer conformity with care

Addiction and bipolar disorder may interfere with the capacity of an individual to conduct daily tasks and roles of community normally. Homelessness, financial problems, job issues or homelessness, problems with ties, legal problems, and personal interconnections and attempts at suicide are all possible causes of both bipolar disorder and addiction.

Drugs in infancy or puberty may have lasting consequences before the brain is fully grown. According to the National Institute for Drug Abuse (NIDA), it is associated with an increased risk of conditions that will occur later and can be related to an increased risk for later development of other mental health disorders. Mental illness is a child or teenager can also increase the risk of subsequent alcohol use and the initiation of disease.

Co-Occurring Disorder Treatment Complications

Depending on a National Drug Use and Health Survey in 2017, it has been reported that more than 18.7 million people over the last year have been impacted by a drug use problem and more than 8.5 million have had both a substance use issue and mental illness over the course of the past year. This means that about 45% of adults with a substance use disorder in the past year also had mental illness in the past year. Integrated care for people with co-occurring conditions to tackle both psychiatric and alcohol use problems gives better outcomes.

Some substances, such as alcohol, can suddenly be life-threatening. As a consequence, certain patients may need to detox in a hospital outpatient detox unit. Vital signs and mental health can be tracked constantly during inpatient therapeutic detox. Medicines may be used to prevent and/or to provide a more comfortable experience of dangerous complications. Bipolar disorder people may also need drugs to control their condition.

Relapse rates for the use of drugs are strong, NIDA reports between 40 which 60% and may even be greater for those with co-occurring disorders. When previously discussed, peoplewith co-occurring bipolar disorder and substance use disorder often have poorer clinical outcomes and findings than just bipolar disorders.

Co-occurring bipolar disorder and substance use disorder are recommended to be treated simultaneously by professionals in an integrated form. Although no method of care has been created for co-occurring bipolar disorder, the treatments include psychotherapy, drugs used to manage conditions of alcohol use, and/or medications for curing bipolar disease. Peoplewith co-occurring bipolar disorder and drug use disorder can learn to manage their disorders and to live healthier, happier lives in collaboration with care providers.

THE DIFFERENCE BETWEEN BP-1 AND BP-2

Bipolar disorder is abnormally high and, in some cases, low mood mental health condition. It affects the energy levels of a person and their ability to function in daily life.

There are different types of bipolar disorder, the most prominent being bipolar I and bipolar II.

Bipolar I Vs. Bipolar II

Bipolar I and II have signs and cycles of symptoms that are identical. People with bipolar II, though, will have less extreme manic episodes than those with bipolar I. This mania is called hypomania.

To be diagnosed with bipolar II, a patient must also have a major depressive episode, which is not necessary in the case of bipolar I diagnosis.

A physician may diagnose bipolar I on the basis of a manic episode alone. Persons of bipolar I disease have at least one manic episode lasting for a week or more or extreme mania involving admission.

In fact, people with bipolar II disorder do not require hospitalization during hypomanic times. Physicians often misdiagnose bipolar II as a disorder because it can be very mild with hypomanic symptoms.

Between these episodes of mania and depression, people with these kinds of bipolar may have stable moods. Symptoms of depression and mania can also occur at the same time. This is termed psychotic or "mixed features."

Symptoms

Depression, hypomania, and insomnia are the primary signs in bipolar I and bipolar II.

Mania

People can experience during a manic episode:

- ✓ Intensive energy or joy or anticipation
- ✓ Energy described as over-talking or overactive
- ✓ Needless sleep and difficulties of sleeping
- ✓ Thought about sleeping
- ✓ Discernment, focus on decision making
- ✓ Reckless actions
- ✓ Pleasure-seeking behavior, such as elevated female desire, drugs and alcohol

✓ High self-esteem

Mania cycles may interfere with the daily activities and relationships of an individual with others.

Many people may not be able to enter a stable state or to think rationally during a manic episode.

Hypomania

In hypomania, individuals experience symptoms similar to mania, except less severe.

Hypomania can still affect the quality of life of a person, and family and friends can find that the person experiences mood changes.

Depression

People with bipolar disorder may have depressive symptoms close to those associated with clinical depression. It includes:

    ✓ Sadness
    ✓ Hopelessness
    ✓ Low energy and fatigue
    ✓ Changes in sleeping patterns
    ✓ Changes in appetite
    ✓ Poor concentration

- ✓ Loss of interest in formerly enjoyable activities
- ✓ Low self-esteem
- ✓ Aches and pains that have no apparent physical cause
- ✓ Thoughts of suicide or death
- ✓ Suicidal behavior

Physicians see these signs as depression because they last for 2 weeks or longer.

Prevalence

In the United States, approximately 2.8 percent of adults suffer from bipolar disorder in a given year, according to the National Institute of Mental Health (NIMH). Approximate 4.4 percent of people at some point in their life develop psychotic. The disease nearly similarly impacts men and women. Evolution occurs at an average age of 25 years but may occur to people of any age.

Diagnosis

To be diagnosed with bipolar disorder, a doctor or a counselor will be required. You must analyze the medical history and symptoms of the individual.

This psychiatric evaluation relies on the emotions, feelings, and actions of an individual.

Many people might find it useful to have a loved one there, particularly during stressful periods, to remind the doctor about other symptoms. The therapist or counselor may also ask a person to hold their moods, sleep habits, and other symptoms in their journal. This diary is valuable for a diagnosis. The doctor or physician equate the effects of the individual to the diagnostic and predictive manual of mental disorders (DSM-5) guidelines for bipolar disorders. The doctor or counselor can conduct blood tests, physical exams, or brain imaging scans to diagnose certain symptom triggers.

Treatment

Bipolar I and bipolar II disorders are typically treated with medications, psychotherapy, and changing lifestyles. Since bipolar disorder is a long-term illness, treatment will be enduring. Many patients may have a treatment team, including a counselor, therapist, and doctor.

Medications

Physicians usually prescribe mood stabilizers for bipolar disorder, such as creatine. We may also recommend antipsychotic medications for manic episodes and depression antidepressants.

Because antidepressant medicines in some patients may "cause" manic episodes, physicians may prescribe a combination of antidepressant drugs and antipsychotic drugs to minimize depression while maintaining mood stable.

Anti-anxiety drugs, such as benzodiazepines, can help people with anxiety or sleep problems. This strategy may, however, involve a risk of benzodiazepine dependence. People can start taking medications right away, even if a bipolar or suicidal disorder does not actually exist. It is important that drugs proceed even during times of calm mood to avoid recurrence.

Psychotherapy

Psychotherapy is an essential part of bipolar I and II treatment. Therapy can take place independently, in a group, or in a family environment.

Various types of counseling may be effective, including:

✓ Behavioral and social pattern therapy (IPSRT) to help people cope with symptoms.

- ✓ Behavioral therapy (CBT) to counter and remove negative thoughts.
- ✓ Family-oriented counseling, to improve contact and care for family members.

Lifestyle Changes

In order to treat their problems and to regulate their moods, many individuals will modify their way of life. Types of valuable modifications include:

- ✓ Exercise on a regular basis
- ✓ Eating a balanced diet
- ✓ Building up sleep routines
- ✓ Support to a mood-related disorders support group
- ✓ Exercise attention and meditation
- ✓ Reduce stress, wherever possible
- ✓ Learning more about the condition

It is also important for some people to keep a regular attitude log. Keeping a journal can allow people in their thoughts, moods, and behaviors to see patterns.

A mood diary also supports the identification of manic or depressive episodes triggers. This can encourage an individual to take appropriate measures before a slight change of mood worsens.

DISCRIMINATION A SUFFERER MAY FACE

In The Workplace

According to the National Institute for Mental Health, nearly 14 million Americans experience some form of bipolar disorder. There are several forms of bipolar disorder. Each category is defined according to the Depression and Bipolar Support Group by the duration, frequency, and trend of symptoms of mania and depression. Bipolar disorder is covered as a state and federal medical disability

Is Bipolar A Disability?

According to Manic-Depressive.net, bipolar disorder causes disability–both psychiatric and medical–during the depressed phase of the illness. Workers with periods of depression can experience significant cognitive difficulties, which can limit their ability to do basic work and, in some situations, contribute to short-term disability.

Equality Act Of 2010

You can't discriminate as a business owner against a bipolar disorder employee. The Equality Act of 2010 safeguards workers from discrimination on the grounds of age, handicap, class, ethnicity, religion or belief, sex, sexual orientation, employment, civil partnership, and pregnancy and maternity. You can face a job discrimination claim when you terminate or demote an individual based solely on his / her impairment.

Under the American Disability Act, the word "disability" applies to a physical or mental condition that greatly affects or documents that a person has a major life function.

An individual with bipolar disorder should be granted days off to prepare for different drugs ' side effects or attend therapy sessions or physicians ' appointments. If the illness of the employee is aggravated by complex tasks, it should take additional time to complete the assignments. If you do not allow these arrangements, the business can be sued for prejudice.

The Equal Employment Opportunity Commission

The Equal Employment Opportunities Commission is a federal agency that safeguards workers from discrimination and harassment at work. The EEOC reviews job discrimination allegations based on race, color, faith, sex (including pregnancy), national origin, or impairment, as defined on its website.

An employee must file a complaint of job discrimination with the EEOC within the period permitted by law. If the case is protected by a state or local anti-discrimination law, the time limit can be extended to 300 days. The employee must demonstrate that he was discriminated against due to his disability if a discrimination suit is to be won. Discrimination can include firing, insufficient working conditions, or harassment.

BIPOLAR DISORDER IN CHILDREN

Any parent knows that without warning, a child's temperament, attitude, caring, or energy level will shift. Nevertheless, these improvements sometimes do not reflect the maturity age of a child nor suggest that a child has mental health. When a person has a bipolar disorder, attitudes, which can escalate to a high or low manic episode, defined as a depressed period, are incredibly mood change. In late adolescence or in early adulthood, bipolar disorder is more likely to occur, but children can experience it too. Effective Diagnosis and treatment are important for children to learn how to manage problems and to excel in their lives.

It is believed that bipolar disorder exists in 1-3% of young people, most of whom are adolescents rather than children1. This illness can be difficult to diagnose — it could take doctors many years to monitor the individual and make an accurate evaluation. Bipolar I and Bipolar II are two forms of bipolar disorder. An infant must follow the conditions for a manic episode to obtain a diagnosis of Bipolar I (see below). You may also have distressed periods, but not usually. A kid has both hypoxia (a milder form of mania) and a major depressive disorder to obtain a diagnosis of bipolar II.

Symptoms Of Mania In Children

- ✓ Acting unusually silly or happy
- ✓ Having a short temper
- ✓ Hyperactivity
- ✓ Irritability
- ✓ Talking with rapid speech
- ✓ Trouble sleeping or needing less sleep
- ✓ Trouble concentrating
- ✓ Talking excessively about sex
- ✓ Engaging in risky behaviors2

If the mood is higher and hyperactive than usual, a child may have experienced a hypomanic episode, but the symptoms do not harm him so much that they require hospitalization or impairment at school or at home.

Symptoms Of Depression In Children

- ✓ Feeling very sad or low
- ✓ Lack of interest in playing
- ✓ Complaining about stomachaches and headaches
- ✓ Trouble sleeping or sleeping excessively

- ✓ Over or undereating
- ✓ Expressing feelings of guilt or worthlessness
- ✓ Thinking about death or suicide
- ✓ Trouble concentrating
- ✓ Feeling fatigued

Bipolar Disorder And Disruptive Mood Dysregulation Disorder

Writers in the latest version of the American Psychiatric Association's Diagnostic and Statistical Manual of Mental Disorders (DSM) also added a new developmental mood disorder named Disruptive Mood Dysregulation Condition (DMDD). Kids aged 6 and 18 years of age can be diagnosed with DMDD, and many of the signs of DMDD are close to bipolar disorder. These include bursts of the temperature, irritability, and frustration. A person is not treated with both depression and DMDD, so a clinician needs to find out which treatment describes the signs of the infant in the most accurate way.

ADHD And Bipolar Disorder

The symptoms of ADHD and mania or bipolar disorder can sometimes be very similar. Children could be distracted, talkative, difficult to keep an eye on, and loss of social function. Clinicians need to decide whether this is one disease or if the conditions co-occur. If an infant experiences behavioral disturbances, severe mood swings, and impulsive behaviors, both ADHD and bipolar disorder may be present. If your child is already diagnosed with ADHD and has an exaggerated sense of self, risky sexual behavior, a loss of need for sleep, and self-relief, therefore mania correlated with bipolar disorder may also arise. A child psychiatrist may help exclude other conditions and recommend options for treatment.

Treatment For Bipolar Disorder In Children

Treatment for bipolar disorder children typically involves a mixture of treatment, counseling, psychoeducation, and educational support.

A combination of drugs can include antidepressants, mood stabilizers, antipsychotics, and/or antianxiety drugs. As the minds of children are still growing, doctors suggest that they "start small and go down" when it comes to medicine. Physicians want the least medications and the lowest dosages to give the child the best results.6 Parents must be vigilant because they may need several attempts to find the right medicine for their child. The efficacy of drugs can change as they age.

If you have a concern, ask the doctor of your child, whether an FDA medicine for pediatric use has been approved and whether the results were obtained in clinical trials with children. Parents should also know that there is a small but increased risk of suicide for children and teens taking antidepressants, so it's important to monitor your child's signs.

Therapy is an essential component of bipolar disorder diagnosis. Therapy can help older children learn how to cope with symptoms and develop healthy self-care habits to reduce the risk of drug misuse or other risky behavior. Play therapy can assist younger children to express their ideas and explore positive ways to cope and develop their self-esteem. Above all, children can feel understood and voice their concerns in a therapist's office.

Psychiatric care may be a significant therapeutic factor for both bipolar disorder parents and children. Hospitals, hospitals, classrooms, and other voluntary groups, as well as communities with individuals with bipolar disorders, can provide educational information on mental illness, coping techniques, and management strategies. Support groups can also be a valuable tool for parents who want to know more about mental health and youngsters.

School counseling is important in the care of mentally ill children. If your child is diagnosed with bipolar disorder, it is eligible for an individualized education program (IEP), which adapts the educational experience to its interests, talents, and difficulties. Education counselors, school psychologists, social workers, nurses, and other personnel will help your child excel at educational and beyond.

Alternative treatments are becoming increasingly popular in bipolar disorder treatment. Children participating in meditation have demonstrated improved executive function and flexibility. Additionally, the use of cannabidiol (CBD) oil as a potential alternative treatment for mental illness in children is being gradually investigated. Talk to your doctor about the potential utility and the potential risks and benefits of alternative treatments for your child.

Although it can be easy to feel powerless when a child suffers from bipolar disorder symptoms, the best thing you can do is remain patient and love and support your child. Although an accurate diagnosis can take time, realize that different forms of treatment will make a huge impact on a child's life in the meantime. If your child is facing any of these symptoms, consider learning more about the mental health challenges of your child and opportunities for helping them to achieve their full potential in life. Bipolar disorder can be treated, and individuals with bipolar disorder can live healthy and happy lives.

UNDERSTANDING MANIA AND HYPOMANIA

Mania and hypomania are periods in which a person feels very active, energetic, and active. Hypomania is a less intense style.

Mania and hypomania both occur during periods when the person is excited or energetic. They differ in the severity of these changes in mood:

- ✓ Último Mania is a severe episode that can last a week or more. An individual can feel overwhelmingly elated and very energetic. These symptoms interfere with everyday life, and a person may have to be hospitalized in severe cases.
- ✓ Towards Hypomania is an event lasting a few days. People may feel really good and work well. Families or associates may detect changes in mood or behavior, while the hypomanic individual can not.

The most common connections to mania and hypomania are bipolar disorder. They also can occur in other mood conditions, such as schizoaffective disorder.

Bipolar disorder is a mental health disorder in which a person has changes in mood, energy, activity, and thinking.

People with bipolar I disorder experience mania, while people with bipolar II disorder experience gastrointestinal disease.

Symptoms Of Mania

Incontrovertible excitement, high energy levels, over-confidence, and a lack of social inhibitions can be symptoms of mania.

The madness goes beyond usual moods and shifts in strength. The symptoms are so severe that the relationships, work, or well-being of a person can be affected.

Madness doesn't always mean the person's joy. While mania can trigger euphoria, it can also cause extreme irritability.

Mania signs may include:

- ✓ A Controllable Awakening
- ✓ They feel very happy or elated
- ✓ A Feeling irritable or very chaotic
- ✓ High levels of stress that people find it impossible to manage

- ✓ High levels of behavior, such as repetitive jumping, fidgeting or agitation
- ✓ Difficulty paying attention or concentrating
- ✓ Unrealistic self-esteem and very strong self-confidence.
- ✓ A lack of inhibitions in society
- ✓ For racing thoughts
- ✓ No need to sleep or not to sleep
- ✓ Risk-taking or reckless actions
- ✓ Suicide or self-harm thoughts

Psychotic symptoms may arise during an episode of mania. These could include:

- ✓ Great illusions, or think they are unbeatable, very strong, or popular
- ✓ Hallucinations or objects are seeing or hearing, which are not there.

In the NIMH, manic episodes in bipolar disorder lasts at least 7 days or for any period if the symptoms are so extreme that the individual is required for hospital treatment. Between episodes, the patient may have normal feelings or mild, recurrent symptoms.

Symptoms Of Hypomania

Hypomania is a milder mania. Individuals of bipolar 2 disorder include hypomania. When a full manic episode happens, a diagnosis of bipolar 1.

- ✓ Hypomania signs may include:
- ✓ Having a higher, happier mood than usual
- ✓ Higher irritability or gross behavior
- ✓ Higher activity or energy levels than usual without a strong cause
- ✓ A strong physical and mental well-being feeling
- ✓ To be much more social and speechful than usual
- ✓ To be sexually stronger than usually
- ✓ Sleeping less than usual

How Are They Diagnosed?

The doctor will probably take a medical history and perform a physical exam during your visit. You need to tell your doctor about all prescription, over-the-counter (OTC) medicines and supplements and any illicit medicines you may have taken.

Depression and hypomania can be difficult to treat. For example, you may not be aware of certain symptoms or how long you have them. Sometimes, if you have insomnia because the psychiatrist doesn't recognize depressive or hypomanic tendencies, instead of bipolar disorder, they will treat you with depression.

However, certain aspects of health can induce mania and hypomania. Furthermore, an overactive thyroid gland may cause symptoms of hypomania or mania.

1. Diagnosing mania– Signs must last at least a week in most instances to be classified as mania by the doctor. But if your symptoms are so severe that you are in the hospital, even if the symptoms last for a shorter time, a diagnosis can be made.

2. Diagnosing hypomania-For the diagnosis of hypomania, you must have at least four days with three of the symptoms listed above in "Symptoms."

Differences

Mania and hypomania share several symptoms. The frequency of these signs is a distinctive element.

Mania and hypomania also include shifts of attitude and actions above normal, regular changes.

Mania is so severe that the usual activities of a person can not continue. In more extreme cases, immediate hospital care may be needed.

A person with hypomania can continue as usual. Family and friends can note this even though the person doesn't know it is the individual behaving differently. However, they must still seek medical help to prevent symptoms from deteriorating.

While hypomania is not as severe as mania, it can also be dangerous and have negative implications for the overall well-being of a person.

One study found that during hypomanic episodes, people are more likely to engage in risky behavior. This included waste of resources, improper use of alcohol or drugs, dangerous driving, or risky sexual activity.

Madness but not hypomania can also contribute to paranoia, visions, or delusional stupor.

If an individual is not handled adequately for hypomania, he or she could become psychotic, but this is not always the case.

Similarities

Late stay and celebrations can cause mania and hypomania.

The symptoms of both mania and hypomania include a very happy feeling, a high emotion, a stronger, more creative feeling. An episode of mania or hypomania can, in some cases, be mixed with one of depression. Specialists call this an episode with mixed elements. If this mix occurs, a person can feel energized, depressed, hopeless, or empty. Many life events or behaviors can trigger a mania or hypomania episode. Such events are alluded to like causes.

A small study of a group of bipolar disorders found that mania and hypomania were triggers:

- ✓ Fallen in love
- ✓ Using recreational medicines, particularly stimulant medication
- ✓ Start a new creative idea
- ✓ Stay late or have a party
- ✓ Go to holidays
- ✓ Listen to loud music

Another study found that mania can also cause the following factors:

- ✓ Stress
- ✓ Lack of sleep
- ✓ Use of antidepressant medicines

When To See A Doctor

If an individual experiences mood changes that are greater than average, a health care provider should be seen. Bipolar disorder can be difficult to diagnose, but it can assist with a detailed health history, physical examination, and explanation of moods and symptoms.

If a friend or family member seems to have signs of mania or hypomania, they should explore seeing a psychiatrist and receiving treatment for someone nearest to them.

Treatment And Prevention

Depression or hypomania are not healed. However, patients can control their problems with medicine and speech therapy. Both therapies can help prevent mania and hypomania as well as depressive episodes.

A person should take his medications as prescribed by a doctor, which is usually continuous to avoid symptoms of mania or depression.

Drugs that can help people with bipolar disorder include:

- ✓ Mood stabilizers include antidepressants and antiseizure medications
- ✓ The second generation, or atypical antipsychanisms for mania and hypomania
- ✓ Antidepressants, which in some situations may be effective when managing depressant symptoms with bipolar disorder
- ✓ Sleep treatment may be of little use to those with sleeping problems.

A combination of medication and talk therapy is useful to many people. Often known as psychotherapy, talking counseling can provide bipolar disorder care, encouragement, and awareness.

People taking mania or hypomania should not stop taking this medicine without talking to their doctor. Stop medication suddenly may lead to more severe symptoms when mania returns. A person may also have dangerous symptoms of withdrawal.

While improvements in the lifestyle can not cure mania and hypomania alone, people can try to control their symptoms and possibly avoid triggers:

- ✓ Eat a healthy diet, and avoid skipping food.
- ✓ Practice good sleep hygiene. Go to bed and wake up every day, if possible, at the same moment. Stop staying late and make the sleep schedule flexible every day.
- ✓ Hold an attitude shift log or use a mood map. This can help a person to detect mania or hypomania so that they can interact with the doctor and handle it.
- ✓ Keep meetings and take medications as recommended by the doctor.
- ✓ Seek help immediately with self-harm or suicidal thinking.

How To Recognize A Manic Or Hypomanic Episode

It's a good idea to know the signs and symptoms of the disease if someone you meet is or can be bipolar. Yes, if everyone encounters a relative, family member, or even a coworker experiencing such effects, they should be conscious of some indicators of mania and hypomania.

It is not purely scientific to recognize the symptoms of mania. Mania symptoms or even hypomania can be a medical emergency, as can breathability symptoms, chest pain, or bleeding.

It is not necessary to know all the signs and symptoms of bipolar disorder or the diagnostic criteria. Next, we would discuss some of the more regular and noticeable symptoms that you can see if a friend or family member is to experience mania. Then you may recommend to the spouse that they contact their doctor or call for emergency medical assistance, depending on the severity of the symptoms.

MAJOR DEPRESSION IS HELL

Manic depression is more than a mere change of the mind. You are witnessing a drastic, dramatic change in the depths of emotions. Such shifts appear to be related little to external conditions. In the manic phase or' hot,' you're not satisfied. You're just ecstatic. An extreme depression, the "small" period of the disorder can be accompanied by a great energy outburst. Periods of fairly normal moods between cycles can be experienced. For different people, these cycles are different. It can last days, weeks, or months.

Manic mode signs include an activity that is out of proportion to how you usually work. You feel too good, "top the world," and your happiness will not be changed. You are extremely optimistic. You might even have fantastic illusions. Nothing can prevent you from doing anything you want. Nothing can go wrong, possibly. Like the stereotypical drunken sailor, you spend money. Sex is great; you can't get enough, fabulous. You have lost good sense and patience.

This can be so hyperactive that you can go with little or no sleep practically for days. You have races insight. It's full of ideas like a brake-free car. During the talk, you turn from subject to subject during the quick-fire mode. You talk too loudly and quickly. Others don't understand you because your words and voice are incoherent and disorganized. Sometimes you may get angry for no reason or when someone says that you have unrealistic plans. This period can last up to three months if not treated. Nevertheless, the suicidal process of the disorder usually begins. The symptoms of this disease phase are identical to the "regular" clinical or major depression.

Although the manic-depressive disorder can be impaired, treatment always reacts well. Because many other conditions can obscure manic depression, a competent medical examination is very critical to you or your loved ones as soon as possible.

What Causes Manic Depression (Or Bipolar Disorder)?

The specific cause of manic depression is not clear, but physiological, hereditary, and psychological causes are assumed to be involved.

1. Biochemistry

Research has shown that this disease is linked to a chemical brain imbalance that can be corrected with appropriate drugs.

2. Genetics / Bipolar

The hereditary disorder tends to occur in families. Studies also established multiple genes that may be related to the condition, meaning that several biochemical complications can exist in bipolar disorders. But, if you have bipolar disorder and your partner doesn't, your child is likely to have just 1 in 7. If you have a number of relatives with bipolar disorder or depression, the chance may be greater.

3. Mania and depression

Are often cyclical and occur at specific times of the year. Changes in hormonal processes, including changes in sleep and hormones, are typical of the disorder. Seasonal shifts are often correlated with stimuli.

4. Psychological stress

Genetically sensitive people can have a faulty' turn off' point–emotional excitement can continue to escalate into mania: backsliding can get worse into a deep depression.

Sometimes a stressful event like a job loss, marital problems, or family death may contribute to an episode of mania or depression. Episodes arise at other times for no apparent reason.

Work is still necessary to identify the symptoms, causes, and ways of treating manic depression more precisely.

The faster the therapy starts, the more effective it can be to prevent future events.

Who Gets Manic Depression?

Manic illness is widespread –impacting about 1% of the population. Men and women are affected equally. While the disorder is seen in children, late adolescence and early adulthood are the usual starting age. Madness arises in the elderly for the first time and is often related to another medical condition. Manic disorder is not limited to any gender, race or nationality, religious or professional. Although the same number of men and women contract the condition, people tend to experience more incidents of manicure. Females have more depressive episodes. Most individuals are well known for bipolar disorder. Some of them have won academy awards; others have created or led their countries in critical times of historical literary and fine art masterpieces.

Very effective treatments are available for bipolar disorders.

Is Manic Depression Treatable?

Fortunately, the answer to this question is "yes." Medication and therapy care can be successful for most individuals with manic depression.

Bipolar disorder is identical to other life-long disorders like high blood pressure and diabetes because it can not be "healed." Nevertheless, it can be treated effectively with proper treatment, which allows most people to return to a productive life.

On the other side, when detected and not managed, the consequences of the disease can be catastrophic for the patient, others, and community as a whole.

Around 85% of those with an original episode of manic depression will have another. Maintenance treatment is, therefore, essential in this disease.

Good quality of life with effective treatment is usually possible.

How Is Manic Depression Diagnosed?

A comprehensive past and background is the secret to a bipolar depression diagnosis. Although the patient is usually the main source of information, the contributions of family members and other people involved may be helpful. If the patient arrives for therapy during an episode of depression, the diagnosis may not be made unless a pattern of prior depressive or hypomanic episodes is found. Since some of the signs of extreme mania and schizophrenia may be identical, the separation between them may be complicated when the whole of the therapeutic phase of the disorder has a detailed history. While no clinical testing diagnosing manic depression are available, other studies may be useful for excluding mental conditions that mimic mania or depression.

How Often Should I Talk With My Doctor?

During acute mania or depression, most people discuss symptoms, doses, and side effects with your doctor at least once a week or even daily. As you recover, the contact becomes less frequent; once you're good, you could see your doctor every few months for a quick review.

Whatever treatments or blood tests are planned, contact the doctor if you have:

- ✓ Suicidal or violent feelings
- ✓ Changes in mood, sleep or energy
- ✓ Changes in side effect medication
- ✓ A need to be used on counter drugs like cold medicine or pain medicine
- ✓ Acute general medical conditions, surgery, extensive dental care, or changes in other medications you take.

What About Hospitalization?

Treatment in the hospital is sometimes required, although usually short (1-2 weeks). Hospitalization may be essential if self-destructive, impulsive, or aggressive behavior is to be prevented that people later regret. Most people still lack insight into their condition and need to be hospitalized. Research has shown that most manic patients, even though they were delivered against their will, are grateful for the help received after recovery. During stress, hospitalization is also used for people with medical complications that make it more difficult to control treatment and for persons who can not stop taking alcohol or drugs. Remember that early recognition and treatment can reduce the chances of hospitalization for manic and depressive episodes.

HOW TO TREAT BIPOLAR DISORDER WITH MEDICATION

Diagnosis

To decide whether you have bipolar disorder, the tests may include:

- ✓ **Towards the physical examination.** Your doctor can conduct a physical examination and laboratory tests to determine any health problems that may trigger your symptoms.
- ✓ **Towards psychiatric evaluation.** Your doctor may refer you to a psychiatrist who will talk about your thoughts, feelings, and patterns of behavior. You can also complete a psychological self-evaluation or questionnaire. Families or close friends may be required to provide details on their symptoms with your consent.
- ✓ **After mood charting.** Charting a daily record of your moods, sleep patterns, or other factors may be required to help diagnose and find the right treatment.
- ✓ **Bipolar disorder definition.** Your psychiatrist may compare your symptoms

with the criteria for bipolar and related disorders in the American Psychiatric Association's Diagnostic and Statistical Manual of Mental Disorders (DSM-5).

Diagnosis In Children

While the treatment of the bipolar disorder, children, and adolescents requires the same guidelines for adults, children's and young adolescents ' manifestations frequently vary and may not fall into the diagnostic categories properly.

For comparison, adolescents with bipolar disorder are often also treated with other mental health conditions such as ATDS or behavioral problems that can hinder treatment. A reference to a child psychiatrist with bipolar disorder experience is recommended.

Treatment

Therapy is best guided by a medical doctor who is an expert on the diagnosis and treatment of bipolar and related conditions (psychiatrist). It may include a counselor, a social worker, and a psychiatric nurse.

Bipolar disorder is a lifelong disorder. Treatment is aimed at symptom management. Treatment may include, depending on your needs:

- ✓ **Towards drugs.** You will often need to begin taking medicines to balance your moods immediately.
- ✓ **Continued treatment.** Towards continued treatment. Bipolar disorder needs continuous medical care, even when you feel better. People who miss maintenance therapy are extremely at risk of symptom recurrence, or mild moods transform into full mania or depression.
- ✓ **Night recovery services.** Weekend care facilities. A day treatment program may be prescribed by the doctor. Such services provide the help and advice you need while monitoring symptoms.
- ✓ **Treatment of substance abuse.** You will also need to be monitored for drug abuse if you have problems with alcohol or medications. Otherwise, bipolar disorder can be very difficult to manage.
- ✓ **For Hospitalization.** If you're dangerous, feel suicidal or get rid of reality (psychotic), your doctor may recommend hospitalization. Psychiatric treatment in a hospital can help you to stabilize and calm

your mood, regardless of whether you have manic or depressed episodes.

Medicines and psychiatric counseling (psychotherapy) for managing effects are the main therapies for bipolar disorder, as well as education and support services.

Medications

Several drugs are used to treat bipolar disorder. The drug forms and dosage are focused on your specific symptoms.

Drugs may include:

- ✓ **Towards stabilizers of Mood**. To order to control depressive or hypomanic episodes, you typically require mood-stabilizing medications. For example, lithium (Lithobid), valproic acid (Depakene), divalproex sodium (Depakote), carbamazepine (Tegretol, Equetro, others) and lamotrigine (Lamictal) are the examples.
- ✓ **Towards antipsychotics.** When, following certain drugs, symptoms of depression or mania continue, an antipsychotic drug such as olanzapine, risperidone, quetiapine

(Seroquel), aripiprazole (Abilify), ziprasidone (Geodon), lurasidone (Latuda), and asenapine (Saphris) may be effective. Some of these drugs may be prescribed by your doctor alone or with a mood stabilizer.

✓ **Against antidepressants.** The psychiatrist should prescribe an opioid to help control the depression. Since an antidepressant may sometimes cause a manic episode, a cognitive stabilizer or antipsychotic is usually prescribed.

✓ **The antidepressant-antipsychotic section.** Symbyax combines fluoxetine antidepressant with olanzapine antipsychotic. This acts as a treatment for depression and a mood stabilizer.

✓ **Anti-anxiety medications.** Benzodiazepines may lead to anxiety and improve sleep but are often used for a short period of time.

Finding The Right Medication

Finding the right drug or drugs would probably take certain checks and mistakes. If you don't fit right, there are a few more to do.

The process requires diligence because it takes weeks to months for certain drugs to take full effect. For a fact, only one drug is modified at a time, and the doctor can figure out which drugs function to ease the problems with the least disturbing side effects. Medicines may also need to be adjusted as symptoms change.

Side Effects

Small side effects also change as you find the right medications and dosage that function for you and adapt your body to the drugs. Talk to your doctor or qualified mental health if you have troubling side effects.

Don't make any changes or stop taking medicines. You may have withdrawal effects, or the symptoms may worsen or return if you stop your medication. You may feel very depressed, suicidal, or go into an episode that is manic or hypomanic. Call your doctor if you think you need to make a change.

Medications And Pregnancy

A variety of bipolar disorder medications may be linked to birth defects and may go to your infant by breast milk. In breastfeeding, other drugs such as valproic acid and sodium Divalproex should not be used. Birth control medicines can also lose their effectiveness when taken together with certain medications for bipolar disorders.

Talk to your doctor about treatment options before you start

Other Treatment Options

Additional treatments may be added to your depression therapy, depending on your needs.

Electric currents pass through the brain during electroconvulsive therapy (ECT), intentionally triggering a brief seizure. ECT appears to cause brain chemistry changes, which may reverse symptoms of certain mental illnesses. ECT may be an option for depression care if you don't progress with medications, whether you can't take medication for health reasons, including abortion or if you have a significant risk of suicide.

Transcranial magnetic stimulation (TMS) is being studied as an option for antidepressants.

Treatment In Children And Teenagers

Treatment is generally decided on a case-by-case basis for children and teenagers based on symptoms, side effects of treatment, and other considerations. Treatment usually includes:

- ✓ **Towards drugs.** Bipolar disorder, children and adolescents are often treated for the same medications as adults. Evidence on the safety and effectiveness of depressive drugs is less common in adolescents than in adults, and treatment decisions still depend on evidence by adults.

- ✓ **Towards psychotherapy.** Original and long-term therapy can help to avoid the appearance of symptoms. Psychotherapy can help children and adolescents to manage their routines, to develop coping skills, to deal with difficulties in learning, to solve social problems, and to strengthen family ties and communication. And it can help to treat drug abuse problems common in older children and teens with bipolar disorder if appropriate.

- ✓ **Towards psychoeducation.** Psychoeducation can involve learning the symptoms of bipolar disorder and their different behaviors, situations, and appropriate behavioral characteristics of your child's developmental age. Comprehension of bipolar disorder can also help you support your child.

✓ **To Support.** Talking alongside teachers and school counselors and promoting family and friends engagement will help to identify programs and promote progress.

HOW TO TREAT BIPOLAR DISORDER WITH THERAPY

Bipolar disorder (BD) is a stress-induced disease. Madness and depression episodes can be caused by life events, serious family disputes, volatile ties, and circumstances that interrupt patterns of sleep and wake. This is why treatment, as mainly pharmacological, is problematic. Those with BD are best able to receive medication management from a doctor and daily psychotherapy (weekly or biweekly).

Therapy can help a person relieve depression, control their symptoms, and strengthen interactions. These are external factors. Several forms of therapy have been found to be effective for BD here.

1. Family-focused therapy-Family-focused therapy (FFT) involves a person and family members with the BD. FFT normally lasts around 12 sessions provided by one therapist (depending on the family's needs). The early sessions focus on education on the disease: the effects and how they change over time, its origins, how early warning signals of new episodes are understood, and what to do, as a team, to avoid episodes from worsening. Further workshops concentrate on empathy and the ability to solve challenges, in particular, to resolve family disputes. We have seen in several randomized studies conducted by my laboratories at the University of Colorado and UCLA that people with BD who receive FFT and medicine following an episode have less severe mood symptoms and function better over 1 to 2 years compared to people receiving medicines, short treatments or case management.

2. Interpersonal and social rhythm therapy- Is a clinical procedure in which a person with a BD retains regular logs of their bedtime, waketime, and behaviors and the impact of shifts in these patterns on their moods. interpersonal and social pattern counseling The clinician teaches the individual how his daily routines and sleep-wake cycles are managed as a way to stabilize moods. The person and his / her therapist identify one or more interpersonal problem areas (e.g., coworkers ' conflicts; friendly difficulties), and discuss possible solutions to prevent similar future problems.

3. Cognitive-behavioral therapy- Cognitive behavioral therapy (CBT) is a psychological therapy that works on the connection between beliefs, emotions, and actions of a client. CBT is teaching people:

- ✓ Identify negative assumptions and habits of thought and encourage ourselves to rehearse constructive ways of thinking.
- ✓ Track their stress levels to make sure that they are deeply affected and that they are not so stressed when they are agitated.

4. Dialectical behavior therapy-Dialectical behavior therapy involves both client and group therapy. This provides cognition and expertise of tolerance, such as the capacity to perceive feelings, impulses, and their corresponding physical sensations from an observer's perspective without critical judgment. It also provides information regarding pain resistance, anger regulation, and behavioral performance.

5. Community psychoeducation–Individuals with BD (often assisted by family members) gather together and are led by a community facilitator (either a consultant or a trained peer counselor). Many classes are highly structured and adopt a program for education and training. Others focus on telling the story and receiving support and suggestions from people who have experienced similar situations. Such programs, including NAMI and the Depression and Bipolar Community Group, are very beneficial for people because they alleviate feelings of isolation that are often correlated with mental illness.

With time, a specific treatment form may not be as important as having a psychiatrist or a community who understands you well and who makes you feel confident enough to discuss major issues. When addiction to drugs, help from mental health professionals who recognize the experience is crucial to a successful treatment and recovery program.

HOW TO TREAT BIPOLAR DISORDER NATURALLY

Bipolar disorder needs two different categories of signs to be treated. Manic symptoms can include impulsive behavior, excessive irritability, and anxiety, while the National Institute of Mental Health reports that depressive symptoms can include low mood, poor appetite, and emotional indifference. While there are not many CAM treatments for manic behavior, a few non-prescription medications may help to ease depression. The National Institutes of Health states that most people with bipolar conditions spend most of their time anxious rather than psychotic.

But it doesn't suggest that people with bipolar disorder can abandon their medications just because of CAM treatments work. "Bipolar is a very serious lifelong disorder," says Philip Muskin, MD of the Columbia University Medical Center, New York City Professor of Psychiatry. You can try the opioid if you are in need. These other kinds of medications are extra or rather similar than a substitute.' The interventions that have shown any value to the depressive aspect of bipolar disorder are supportive and non-pharmacological:

1. Rhodiola-This plant, commonly referred to as RhodiolaRosea, has been used for years to help manage stress and has had beneficial effects on people with depression. While Rhodiola does not alleviate distress to the degree that an antidepressant is able, according to a study published in Phytomedicine in 2015, there are fewer side-effects. "Rhodiola is highly relaxing," says Dr. Muskin. "I wouldn't use it as a therapeutic treatment, but it is a good supplement to someone who is on medication and thinks like they[still] don't have much strength."

2. Same-Same or S-adenosylmethionine is a natural body coenzyme, which has been studied widely and shown to reduce symptoms of people who are suffering from major depressive disorders, according to a 2015 study of the CNS & Neurological Disorders— Drug Targets report. However, the same should be used with care with individuals with a bipolar disorder who are stressed because they can actually cause mania, according to the NCCIH. It should only be used under the direct supervision of a doctor.

Anything that's a real medication will induce bipolar mania,' Muskin said.' There is some possibility that an individual will become psychotic.' Many clinical studies are now in development to identify the best method of using it in people with both depression-related and bipolar conditions.

3. St. John's worth-This herb, frequently used in mood management in Europe, is one of the best-known natural mood improvers. Even so, there are conflicting reports of the positive effect of St. John's word on major depression or bipolar disorder. The NCCIH notes that St. John's term may assist with depression but can also contribute to paranoia, and the department reports that it might interfere with many others who have bipolar illness. St. John's wort has shown similar side effects with certain antidepressant drugs as it appears to have a similar effect on the body, according to the 2015 Clinical and Experimental Pharmacology and Physiology research journal.

4. Meditation-People who meditate on cognitive treatment based on supervised consciousness can see a reduction in depression that directly correlates to how many days they meditate. According to a study published in 2013 in Behaviour Science and Therapy, the fewer effects they meditate.

5. Omega-3 fatty acids-Individuals with bipolar disorder may be inspired to consume more antioxidants in omega-3s, such as tuna, mackerel, and sardines, or they may wish to consider omega-3 additives. This is because, according to research published in the American College of Nutrition Review in 2015, the anti-inflammatory properties of omega-3 fatty acids may help regulate the mood. The application of approximately 300 mg Omega-3s every day to a depression program will improve outcomes, according to research published in Polish Psychiatry in 2012. "The prevalence of the bipolar disorder is relatively low if you look at countries where people eat a lot of seafood," Muskin notes. "We agree that omega 3s in the brain will help to move neurotransmitters in and out, helping to balance moods."

6. Light therapy-People with bipolar disorder can have disrupted circadian rhythms, indicating they don't function properly everyday. According to a 2012 review published in Dialogs in Clinical Neuroscience, a number of strategies can be used to reset this internal clock and improve bipolar management. These include time-consuming exposure to light and dark periods and a forced sleep change. If you pursue them yourself, please discuss these or related approaches with your doctor.

7. Traditional Chinese medicine-This method relies on certain plant varieties and extensive nutritional and everyday behavior improvements. There is still insufficient evidence to support or exclude Chinese herbals, a review published in

Evidence-Based Complementary and Alternative Medicine in 2013 concludes. Nonetheless, other types may gain from mood disorders. Consult with a physician with your physicians qualified in the area.

8. Interpersonal and social pattern therapy-This approach helps bipolar to have a more regular schedule for all aspects of life, including sleep, work, food, and exercise. According to a study published in 2015 of bipolar disorders, everyday activity has been increased.

8. Desensitization of the eye movement and reprocessing treatment-A supervised eye movement program combined with an active reminder of traumatic experiences is used to improve symptoms. According to research published in 2014 in the journal Psychiatric Studies, this method can be helpful for people who have bipolar disorder and abuse experience.

Complementary Bipolar Treatments: A Few Words Of Caution

"The reality is that there are not much data on bipolar disorder complementary therapies," says Muskin. This does not mean that these products shouldn't be used, but that patients shouldn't expect to be able to go to websites like the New England Journal of Medicine and download a lot of the books when they try to find out about them.' "You will ask if the substance you purchase includes the commodity you believe it does or not, and what it is labeled for and if it has toxins," he says. The National Institutes of Health Office of Dietary Supplements also provides detailed product and manufacturer information in an extensive online database of dietary supplements.

Most of these drugs are effective, and adverse associations with prescription medicines are restricted. Patients and their families may, however, carefully research these drugs and discuss options with their physicians, particularly when complementary therapies do not require the same stringent testing as prescription medicines.

REAL LIFE STORIES

Personal Stories

My Story With Bipolar Disorder

I can honestly say that I had no discernible signs of mental illness until the end of college. It all started at the end of my college week in the second to last quarter. I was 23. I was 23. Before spring break, I had one final examination left. After the spring quarter, I was scheduled to graduate.

I've been second in my civil engineering class. A classmate met me in the end week at a bar for a pitcher of green beer. I saw the bartender mix the green food into the beer. The remaining thing that happened that day is a blur. And not a blur in the case of "I got drunk and blacked out," but a blur where my friend claimed I felt like I had 30 drinks as I walked back into the apartment. I didn't even finish the pitcher, in fact.

I remember feeling like my arms were on fire and a rush of adrenaline. I recall my hands shaking a lot, and for the first time in my life, a lot of anxiety. I struggled through the final because I didn't feel right physically.

The sensation lasted for the spring break on the way home from Athens to Canton. The adrenaline rush started, the anxieties intensified, and I couldn't keep still. My mind raced. The drive home was like a lifetime. I always wanted to get home and tell my parents what happened and maybe go to an emergency room.

I came home and wasn't able to sleep or still stay at all. The fear has grown. I couldn't even sit down and watch tv. My mother and her boyfriend figured the green beer I consumed might have been lacquered. All we thought was false, so they took me to the emergency room. In the packed waiting room, I vaguely remember screaming political comments while I waited. I've been checked into the local mental hospital.

I wasn't comfortable most of the time in solitude. I started to have delusional grandeur fantasies. Like, perhaps I was here for a crime that I don't remember committing? My imagination began to play games on me. I lost track of time completely. This feels like I've been in the room for months. I saw only the nurses and my psychiatrist for days. They started giving me routine medication, but I recall refusing it for the first few days. I was wondering, and narcotics brought me into this mess, how could they get me out? Then a nurse told me about the sixth time to take my medication , and

I said no. She said then, "Wouldn't you like to go home?"Home. Home. I didn't even remember what it was at school. My mind had been going at 200 mph for about 4 to 5 days, so I didn't remember that my father and I had a house around the corner of this facility.

It was then that I stopped taking medicine and began to recover gradually. It was then treated as a drug-induced psychosis, possibly by consuming PCP-laced alcohol. My doctor probably said it was "one-time." I continued on my prescription medications for the best part of a year. Throughout Spring 2007, I did not return to college throughout time to graduate as I had expected. I wanted the quarter to heal emotionally. Yet I came back to my last quarter of undergraduate classes in fall 2007. As I was returning, my doctor said that I was doing well enough to wean me from my medication slowly. This turned out that just after I came back to the university, I was again free of drugs, for better or for worse.

I still had a successful final quarter and graduated with a Bachelor of Science Cum Laude in Civil Engineering in November 2007. Before that, I agreed that I also wanted to attend a civil engineering graduate school in the next quarter in winter 2008. I was curious and very interested to see what went into engineering research.

Everything was new to me. I had been away from my medicine for a long time now and began to recur while I began college. I began to lose sleep again. I started to have grandiose plans for the design and construction of my own home. I began to have thinking about driving transformed into religious delusions. During those moments, I start thinking that many various illusory ideas are actually real, and I was stupid not to think this way before. I recall talking about religion on my best friend's ear on the line. Night after night, sleep was lost before I eventually panicled my mom and asked her something was wrong. She drove me to the campus and took me to the local psychiatric ward once again.

My second episode was more serious. I've had great paranoid delusions, thinking I've been the Antichrist or the messiah or both. I believed that the news channels broadcast me lived on TV when the messiah / antichrist was there for the whole world in a local hospital. I thought that everyone in the hospital hated me and everyone watching the news. I have had numerous auditory hallucinations, from my classmates and teachers to God.

This episode, again, was misdiagnosed as a second psychotic episode and a single incident. I was also misdiagnosed. I had to leave graduate school, never complete a quarter.

I stayed on medicine for much longer and was even good enough to work in an engineering firm for a year and a half. Instead, I planned to go to school near the house. It went well despite my mental state being depressed and confused. I have a Masters of Civil Engineering and have completed a paper of 140 words. But once again, another physician finally claimed I was okay and weaned my medicine right after graduation in May 2012.

All this stress caused my third and most serious manic episode. Life moved too quickly for me, even though I had no insight. I scared my mother while I was staying with her. I began to lose sleep again. Once I missed traveling to Canton from Cleveland, a trip that I memorized. I was unfit to drive and had a severe car crash. In a week, I lost my job, lost my boss and best friend, and on my 27th birthday in December 2012, I was referred to a local psychiatrist.

That period was an intense mania and was not only during my hospital stay. It included the fistfight with my dad, an altercation with Cleveland police, very dangerous behavior, grandiose thoughts, retail chat, and listening experiences as I closed my eyes, like strobe lights, visualizers, and even ufos.

Finally, I was officially diagnosed with a severe bipolar 1 psychotic disorder. All three of my cases were severe psychotic experiences with some insanity. I'm back on medication, this time for good and since, for four years since, the manic episode has been gone. But I want more than self-isolation at home, and I feel deprived at this point in my life. I feel I've got a lot to offer this world.

My future plans include working part-time to see if I can deal with a part-time work burden. I will also qualify for a licensed peer advocate of mental health— because I follow all requirements and certainly have a long-standing mental health background— which can become employment opportunities. My overall objective is to return to civil engineering and start my work. I did it before, so I realize I've got the right cognitive skills and positive people around me to do it again. NAMI support groups helped me understand that in my treatment, I'm not alone. Recovery is possible, I truly believe. My tale has not yet ended. I'm happy for my future to heal.

Liz's Story: Living With Bipolar

Until 2002, when I had insomnia and was given Prozac, I had no history of mental illness. A year after, a series of events caused me to get depressed and psychotic: my relationship ended, I returned to my home, I endured four years of bullying, was fired, and my nose had to be repaired after a sports accident.

I grew "crazy," but at first, my friends nor I felt anything was different because I was always really busy and involved. My manager realized something was wrong and asked my parents to send me to the hospital.

At this point, my mania led me to believe that Jesus ' sister and I were invincible. I was given drugs to decrease my dose because of this mania, but the heavy doses left me really anxious and stayed in the hospital for six weeks.

Bipolar disorder was identified at this time. When I left the hospital, I lived with my parents, and for two weeks, I stopped eating and did not leave my room. This took me the next eight months to get stronger with my stepdad and my mother's support and encouragement.

I returned to my role as an Internet publishing company office manager but found that the mood of my coworkers shifted against me: they didn't know how to respond. They seemed to walk around me on eggshells and didn't know how much work they should give me. My manager started to scrutinize my job and criticize me. Shortly after, I left the company.

In 2004, 2005, 2006, I encountered more manic episodes (in which I felt I'd be the next Queen — Elizabeth III).

Following two and a half years of no more episode in November 2008, I went psychotic because I had to think about my mum, who was sick and didn't sleep for three days. This time, I was very negative and weird, and I recovered quickly: I am convinced that my decision to stop drinking, abandon smoking, and change my lifestyle helped me get through the last attack and recover quicker.

This period, I figured aliens were on the earth, I was battling out of the Matrix those unseen creatures like Neo in 2010. I had my new boyfriend prepared what might happen so that he was all equipped and armed! He took me to the hospital, and I was restful for a week.

I started working with young people with learning difficulties in May 2010 and declared my history in mental health. We were great, and we wanted me for me. It was a genuine eye-opener operating in another area. I take my hat off to carers, and I take it off to carers!

For a year, I did so and went back to work in London. I got very excited again and sensed positive energy surrounding me this time-I wanted to help to change the world again. (Not a bad thing

I guess) I went immediately to see my doctor, and he increased my medication. This took a while to get going, so I paid £ 4,000 on the credit card of my wife-whoops! I quickly recovered and went to work locally–less stress.

I am used to becoming Bipolar over the years, and I am mindful that it will always be part of my life. I do a daily exercise that benefits and has also found community and person therapy sessions very beneficial.

I feel that now is the time to share my story and knowledge in order to reduce the stigma associated with mental health. I want to encourage other people not to make mistakes and know that they have to maintain a healthy lifestyle to control their illness.

Malia's Story

Hello, I'm Malia, a wife, 4-and-a-nurse mother. I'm an RN for 10 years, and I'm working on my master's degree (FNP). It took me years to acknowledge that something was wrong. I've been embarrassed. I'm the patient. I'm a nurse. I should not take the medication myself, and I'm expected to dispense. Initial diagnosis and therapy were initially ROUGH. I have been diagnosed with a bipolar type

I disorder for three years now. I lost weight, didn't sleep well, and my friends noted the shift in me. I hurt for anybody, particularly when their family and friends don't recognize mental illness. I continue to live and embrace what every day is. I seek equilibrium and have a great support system. I am studying harmony.

Chelsea's Story

Chelsea was a married librarian who was 43 years old and came to an ambulatory mental health clinic with a long history of depression. She described herself stressed for one month after she started a new job. He became worried that her new boss and peers found her job to be bad and sluggish, and she wasn't pleasant. At school, she had no strength or passion. She was watching television for hours, overarching, and resting for long hours instead of interacting with her children or communicating with her friends. In just three weeks, she gained six pounds, which made her feel even worse about herself. The week she cried several days, and she said as a warning that "the grief was returning." She, too, often spoke about suicide but never tried to kill herself.

Chelsea had told her recollection of her depressive past that she was a little crazy, and she pulled her husband into her, who remembered her from childhood. We decided that in her childhood, she became unhappy first and that as an adult, she had at least five separate periods of depression. Such periods included deteriorating mood, lack of energy, intense feelings of guilt, loss of interest in women, and some thoughts about life. Often Chelsea also had "too much" strength, irritability, and racing thoughts. Such excess energy events could last for hours, days, or a few weeks.

Chelsea's husband often described moments that Chelsea seemed enthusiastic, happy, and confident– "like another human." She will chat fast, appear full of energy and cheerful, do all the daily tasks, and initiate (and often complete) new projects. She would have to sleep a little and still be awake the next day.

She has seen mental health providers since her mid-teen years, leading to her periods of low mood and feelings of suicide. Psychotherapy provided some assistance. Chelsea said it "worked all right"-until she had yet another episode of depression. Then she couldn't join sessions and just avoided. Four drugs she sought. Growing gave a short-term relief, accompanied by a relapse. An aunt and grandfather were at the hospital for mania, although Chelsea rapidly pointed out that it was "not like them at all." Chelsea had been diagnosed with a bipolar II disorder and had a present depressive episode. Information from her husband about her hypomania helped make the diagnosis.

Claire's Story

When you see someone different, everyone is happy to show the best way to handle this friendship. If you google ' relationship advice,' the internet is packed with similar suggestions.

When I was dealing with a bipolar disorder, I'd often been told things like,' It's better to do nothing' and' do not just confuse it, get to know it first.'

The mental illness problem is that there's no right time to tell that new beautiful friend that you're sick.

I broke all the rules when I met Steve. I spoke to children on our first day, because I didn't want them EVER in my day! Claire Steve, Our second date was much more interesting. (Nor did he, so we were good.) You see, at the height of a hypomanic episode, I started to see Steve. Not a suitable terrain for sex.

The second day was my crash pad night. In the west, all hell broke loose! Pleasant farewell, chatty, smiling, Claire hyperactive.

Hello, devil Claire. Hi Devil Claire.

This evening, I remember very little. I don't even remember how it started. I remember shouting, shouting, throwing, but I couldn't say to who or what. I remembered tossing my hat and bag at the port of Bristol. And then Steve spoke to me off a cliff, actually spoke off a wall, I've been able to go into the water.

And then, after having sat on a bench peacefully after that, I remember him saying a few simple words to me. I'm not worried about what is wrong or how much you are driving me backward, and I'm not going anywhere.

It was in 2007, so he didn't go anywhere. I resisted and pushed at first, not that I didn't like him. Yet I did not deserve somebody so loving and caring as I acted that I did.

How can someone who has been living with this disease deserve so much love? I regretted even taking him through the stress that I put on him.

Over the years, we have learned how to make our relationship work because it's difficult. Steve moves between a partner and a carer. He spends a lot of time checking that I feed, shower, and drink while sadness is in my face. Or just as kindly advise me if I'm hypomanic to slow down a little or try to give' voices' or' visions' to me at the beginning of a psychosis. Despite this, we take time to walk together, hold our hands, talk about everything honestly and openly. We couldn't live if we didn't.

We have problems like every relationship, but my bipolar is a minefield; we are fighting together now, and it makes me more calm and hopeful. The thing I learned from Steve is that it's the best thing you can do to encourage someone to see the weakest component occasionally.

Julianne, 25: "My emotions were so uncontrollably heightened that I wanted to die."

I became hypomanic in middle school. I used my presence carelessly to treat peers and lacked the empathy to know I was harming them. Yet I did succeed in education, worked with several groups, kid school, and was performing in a school band. I wasn't [necessarily] ' acting. ' ' At first, getting schizophrenia was not life-threatening awful.

By the new year[of high school], I drank heavily and took all the herbal drugs that I could find. Yet I didn't care as long as I was attending my honors classes. But at the start of the year, anytime I wanted[to study] or learn something, my mind was running through all the horrible aspects of my life.

My college life was broken without being able to[focus]. I would scream in my pillow every night, shaking and crying. I had so uncontrollably raised my feelings that I wanted to die. I kept telling myself that it would get easier, but for months it happened.

I even began to take scissors to my thighs and felt I should hack off the fat even if I died. I would feel such overwhelming mental pain that I cut and scrap my skin to try to adorn it somehow. I have witnessed hallucinations and paranoia: snakes attacked me on the walls and doors. I wouldn't sleep in a row for days. A month before I was 16, I was diagnosed with bipolar I for children and adolescents at an ambulatory mental health facility.

Well, with fantastic friends, life partners, a home and a career that I'm proud of, I'm a genuinely happy adult. For about eight years, I've been clean of alcohol drugs. But, unless they're close friends, I still don't tell people about my past. The media also portrays people with mental illness as one-dimensional, low-life characters. But their lives have, in various ways, been shattered, and they are only trying to survive. You should not write them off in order to make choices that you do not understand.

Emma, 25: "It drives me crazy, this attitude that mania is a gift that justifies the pain of depression."

I was diagnosed with bipolar II aged 14, after about six years of misdiagnosed ADHD. My doctor referred me to a psychiatrist after she suspected my ADHD to be a misdiagnosis. Now my depression is easier than ever to deal with, partly because it is easier to find community support[more people talk publicly about it]. Madness is still frustrating because it is hard to deal with the after-effects, such as[excessive financial problems] or negative stuff I say or do to those who I care for.

I'm afraid I have kids, which is something I really want to do, too. At least during pregnancy, I would need to be off my medication, if not longer if I breast-feed. In addition to having a child, raising a child is frightening. I would hate my bipolar to affect my relationship with them negatively. I am always looking for optimistic stories of depressive parents who raise children in healthy relationships, but they can be difficult to find. Yet I guess I have a lot of natural curiosity with how others around the planet travel because my actions are sometimes so illogical. I'm able to accept the symptoms of my friends with[mental disease] at face value, and I try without judgment to support them as much as I can.

I agree like Hollywood's most misguided thing about living with bipolar disorder is that mania is a superpower or a blessing. I think of creators produced during the manic, or Carrie (Claire Danes' character) who broke the case in Homeland because of insane savings between rationality and manic. The idea that the world deserves more than the results of bipolar disorder in its own minds is indeed[upsetting]. It scares me nuts because mania is a blessing that excuses the agony of depression. I guess it is hard for people to understand that my insane moments are my most damaging, both in terms of how my life and my interactions are impacted.

Danielle, 29: "The suicidal thoughts that come when I'm down are really tough."

I witnessed frequent mood swings and, retrospectively, serious overreactions about everyday situations before I was treated by my former therapist. I can switch from deep insecurity to super-confidence, and I had thoughts of depression and worthlessness mixed with imagination.

The signs are not really different today, but now I am mature, and I know how to recognize as I hit and can try not to give in. I still have insanely low lows, which last for a few weeks at a time. The suicidal thoughts that come when I'm down are hard. Although, because of my experience with bipolar, I can recognize that as temporary, it does not change that these thoughts are deeply disturbing. The lows are much less familiar to me.

I used to turn to support my loved ones, but I don't want to burden anybody. My dog is always a happy supporter, and journaling and therapy were very effective. Health insurance is currently inaccessible to me, so I have no therapist.

Today, I know I was given a gift often. Bipolar form causes you to confront your feelings. It's not a choice to shoot them down.

Sabrina, 34: "I literally racked up thousands of dollars in debt due to my uncontrollable urge to spend."

I have bipolar NOS, meaning' non-specified.' I do not have bipolar NOS I or II; both are related to my symptoms. I had a long depressive state before I had been diagnosed by a psychiatrist (and then confirmed by a general practitioner), while at the same time being long creative where I felt like I had access to every emotion. I even experienced depression and uncontrollable consumption for more than a decade. I literally racked up thousands of dollars in debt because of my uncontrollable spending urge. I hurt friends and family as I went into depression.

Today my attitude is controlled by alcohol, but it's easier than the lower ones to control the spikes. Most of the time, I also fight low-to-moderate depression. Yet I know I can get engaged with people around me, control my emotions better, and I'm[better at my job]. If my medications are wrong, I can bounce between good days and bad days. When I'm unmedicated, there's no clear' usual.'

I've been working alone for a decade and a half. Most of my near friends are people with whom I talk by computer or phone (and I do it very often). I have a couple of friends from' real life,' but they don't live in the area, so I often talk to them on the phone too. My family is scattered all over the country, so I only see them from time to time, but I'm very close to my mother, and we talk daily. She helps me to keep up tabs on how I look and how I behave. I'm really loyal to my bosses, too.

I want people to know that it's not so' big' as it appears on television. Manic episodes do not necessarily mean hopping or harassing or' funny' people around the home. And bipolar-linked depression does not necessarily manifest as sadness. It's a persistent and pervasive apathy for many men, including myself.

Anna, 23: "Mixed episodes scare me the most. That's where I feel like I completely lose myself."

When I was 19 years old, my doctor diagnosed me with bipolar II. Even with the medication and the coping skills I've acquired, I still have very unpredictable mood swings, but they're not consistently up and down. I have times when I feel' regular,' that is great! But I have had periods of depression and prolonged periods of hypomania in the last five years. I also have mixed episodes where I am severely depressed, but with plenty of energy and restlessness. I keep track of my moods so I can speak if I go into a depression or hypomanic phase.

Alexandra Nyfors Story

As an adult, I'm settled into the first stability I ever had. For the longest time, I have been staying in the same location since I left my childhood home. I am most grateful I decided to live together and very glad that every year from the age of 15 to the age of

53, I was able to pay for social security. Life without pretending is mostly healthy.

A friend of mine read my last book post and sent a note to me. She said, while covering the facts, it didn't really give her a feeling about the isolation of living your life in a hiding place or the marginalization of not hiding. She was right. He was right. My last book was about an intellectual approach. I'll share a few tales for this post.

Hiding my truth

As I said before, I am not only psychotic but also a schizoid. A schizoid is someone for whom social interaction is not the same as for others. We don't like the company. Social activities exhaust us. We want to spend a lot of time at home. We don't feel connected to people like others and don't even normally feel emotions about others. We're essentially within our own heads so much that we just aren't interested.

Imagine me at a Christmas party workplace. This is a small startup of software, approximately 150 people. I'm so uncomfortable that my mind starts buzzing. By wearing a bright blue Hawaiian shirt, I tried to look festive. It's a sad failure, out of step with the themes of Christmas. There's nothing I have to say to anybody else. I made some almost friends at this job, but I'm alone. Without talking to anyone, I spend the entire thing. I eat too much in compensation.

A month later, on one of the servers, I notice a set of photos of the band. They're just me, the fat woman, who feeds. We were apparently passed on as a prank by the company. I'm superficially hurt, but I'm not really irritated or even bothered. I speak to someone with whom I interact, and I'm surprised at their defensive reaction. It transforms into reality. The man who took the pictures and put the joke together is fired, a fallen man who shared for every last manager. I don't feel like part of that stuff, and I don't know somebody I'm dealing with anymore. I remain isolated. I stay isolated.

A few years later, we're going to another Christmas party at another business. I'm in the middle of a deep depressive episode. I can hardly succeed in getting to work and find the desire to be positive and polite for the length of my shift. The idea of getting suited up and going to the workplace on my day off sounds utterly daunting, in light of my previous experience. I know most people love these things. However, I disbelieve them. I don't go. I don't go.

The boss is alive to me. Over the coals, I'm raked. Perhaps for some excuse, the Christmas party was a mandatory occurrence, and I broke a cardinal rule.

Or perhaps I just couldn't hide the fact that I follow the people around me like fish in an aquarium (for those without interest), or at most as protagonists in a book (the interesting). Maybe I have noticed my forced cheer, and they think I hide something more dangerous. We can't talk about it because there is no truth between us. I'm out two weeks later. I'm never going to know exactly.

Not so boldly telling all

I rarely manage to work for more than 18 months or at most two years due to the nature of my illness. A nearly unbeatable mountain is hunting for a job with depression. I have three careers that support them, depending on where I am in functionality. If I work high, I work as a technical writer. I function as a staff accountant or bookkeeper at the middle level. When I'm in a bad state, I'm going to take any kind of work or stuff that I can get, and I haven't done many of them. Put it this way. Put it this way. Those companies are going to hire almost anyone.

A few years after the Christmas debacle, I have the top role in a major software corporation in technical writing. Unfortunately, I sink in a deep depression and am utterly unable to function. I'm taking leave from disabilities. I tell my employer, my handicap personality. She reacts as if, in my spare time, I had confessed to eating babies. She is clearly recoiling. I want to tell her it's not catching, but I don't have the power.

I remain off work for two months on a new combination of medications. Once I quit, I'm not a real person to my team anymore. I am excluded from team projects, e-mail, external outings plans (not a loss of course), and meetings. Certain people won't work for me, either. If I go to speak to someone that I'm supposed to work with, my boss had complained that I have troubled people and wasted their time when I got back to my desk. Such grievances are put to me and sponsored. She sends me a series of accusatory e-mails, where I'm all incompetent, disgusting, and obstructive.

I am ready to kill myself for two months of this treatment. Every last statement I have internalized, and I know that they are all real. The incompetence humiliates me, almost to the point of death. It is by far the worst outcome of any working situation. For a few months, I end up with a long-term disability. In the end, without bias, we decide to split together. They're not going to tell me, and I'm not going to tell them about it.

I'm never going to work again as a technical writer. My life has stopped. I can never again trust in myself enough to look at something and claim, and sure, I can explain how people can use it. I was not only kicked out of college but back to hiding.

Back to basics

From this point on, the work I do and the work I do involve moving to places where I am a stranger, where my references are less likely to be verified. I do everything I can to make a living. There's nothing occasionally. I spend a little time on long-distance buses, then browsing the sofa. That'd be all right if I were 25, but I wasn't that good at 45.

Workplaces tend to have high sales. The building industry is really good for that. Workers generally hire a project or two and then move to another company. Office and support staff continue to be handled in the same manner. It suits my period on time. I'm moving on, inspired, being gold employee, they know something is wrong with me, I'm going. Over and over. Over and over. Following one more layoff, I finally realize that the alternative now is to destroy myself or to quit and find a new way of living. I'm 53 now. I can no longer do it.

I am settled in the first stability I have ever had as an adult five years later. For the longest time since I left my childhood home, I've been stuck in the same location. I'm very glad I decided to live, and I'm extremely grateful that I have been able to pay social security every year from 15 to 53 years of age. Life without pretending is mostly healthy.

So, I can hear you think about it, and everything's about work. How did your personal life change with your disorder? What about friends and family? Okay, that's a completely different kettle of fish, which is another day to wait.

Eleanor's Story

Like so many people who share their stories on this World Bipolar Day, I've lived through bipolar disorder. I'm now 30 years old, but only 16 years of age when I was diagnosed at the Priory Hospital North London with bipolar 1 as the most severe form of mood disorder. At such a young age, it was difficult to address this diagnosis, and then I didn't know what my future would hold. I was admitted to hospital because of three disease episodes: mania and paranoia in a year, which contributed to insanity, where my mind lost contact with reality.

Bipolar is a severe mental illness that causes a mood change either to great manic highs or to devastating depressed lows, with normal working conditions between episodes. I have also encountered depression as an adult with this during my mania, which requires urgent hospitalization, as my mind is completely unstable. Twice (in 2004 and 2014) with my schizophrenia, both times due to an intense case of mania and paranoia, I was treated.

At such a young age, it was difficult to handle this diagnosis, and then I did not know what my future would hold.

I felt sad, nervous, frightened, and weak as a child in a hospital. I (falsely) claimed I was sexually abused, and my life was based on this false belief. The doctors got me back to full health by starting new medications (mood stabilizers) by prescribing me anti-psychotic drugs to get me down from the mania. I also received one or two therapies over four months, group therapy with other youth in the adolescents ' unit, and an incredible team of nurses and a psychiatrist who believed I could do well. I finally went home as soon as my mind became healthy, and a lengthy therapy and recovery process began.

I could go to college and graduate, travel, make friends, anddate and live my life. In 2013, however, I started experiencing depression, after some life stressors, that featured suicidal thinking. It was very disturbing because we think it is because my drug

Carbamazepine was not working when I grew older.

I had group therapy with other adolescents in the youth center and was assisted by an outstanding department of nurses and by a doctor who claimed I could have this type of depression. I stayed in bed all day with meal breaks. I didn't have any motivation, no dream, no reason to get up. I was unmotivated and wasn't able to cope with life. I washed or talked to friends barely. Fortunately, I discussed this with my relatives and the medical team because of my anxiety about suicidal thoughts. I really didn't want to move on it, avoiding the misery in which my head was.

Regrettably, a few months later, the depression turned into a period of mania due to my mood stabilizer, which did not work and took antidepressants. This is always a possibility that medication will take you far. I had chaos, spoke very rapidly, paced emotions, increased libido, and was therefore fragile. The paranoia soon began, with my subconscious falsely believing that my father was being kidnapped by a criminal gang. It was so scary. I have been selected, treated with medication again, and treated at the hospital for several months while trying to restore lucidity to my mood and mind.

My lifeline began with lithium treatment that has controlled my moods for the last five years. Bipolar can be inherited, and my dad does so that there is a potential biological basis, even when science is in its infancy.

The psychosis then began, with my mind beginning to mistakenly believe that I was held by a criminal gang organized by my family. It was so scary.

I have not seen an episode of mania or severe depression since 2014, but I am conscious of the fact that bipolar may occur in the future as recurrent.

I wanted to write this book in the Mental Health Center because I respect their mission of achieving equality in mental health. In this world, we need to reach a balance across mental health confidence, and more funding goes to NHS trusts to hire additional workers to reduce waiting times.

When I became sick at the age of 15 with a depressive case, I applaud the work done by the Institute for children and young people. Most mental illnesses begin as a consequence of life conditions and climate or of a biological connection in communities in childhood or adolescence. It's so important to watch out for signs of anxiety, depression, self-harm, or bipolar disease by caregivers–parents, guardians, and teachers. When you find that a kid has a psychotic or hypomanic episode and is also anxious, you can report it to the GP to send the child to therapy.

 Many mental illnesses start as a result of life circumstances and the environment or a biological link within families during infancy or adolescence.

If it weren't for my parents ' and doctors ' help, today I wouldn't be here. Support for young people (and all ages) with mental illness is vital, and I hope we can highlight this World Bipolar Day.

Eleanor's Story

I began to suffer from depression and anxiety when I was 15. My pulse would pound, I could not relax, and in my GCSE year, it was so poor that I had to take six weeks off classes. I still have my GCSEs, and for a while, I healed. In the following months, however, there was a manic episode and then a depressing episode with psychosis that led me to be voluntarily hospitalized in a teenage mental hospital. At the age of 16, a doctor diagnosed me and my father, a depressive affective disorder.

Bipolar is a serious mood condition that can make patients feel out of control because of signs, with agitation and lower stages lingering several months to depressive, elevated periods.

I'm now 29, but it seemed like a life sentence when diagnosed at 16. I was a quiet girl who tried to belong, and now I had been advised that I would be depressed, that I needed constant medication to keep my moods healthy and keep tabs on them periodically. I didn't know that because of the extent of my condition, the doctors told my parents that they didn't know if I was going to college. I proved it was wrong, but that is what I wanted when I was first diagnosed.

"Not everyone with rapid bipolar cycles."

I'm going between episodes for months, and sometimes there are no Bipolar episodes on my medication. People believe that being bipolar in society means that your mood changes a hundred times a day. That's not the truth. Months and years often go between episodes because everyone with the disorder is special.

Many people cycle quickly in their moods, and it's much slower for others. Let's change the shame.

"You can do whatever you want to do. Just make sure you set realistic goals."

Whether you're going to college, starting a new job, traveling the world–you can do this if you feel good. Make sure you take care of yourself and press for sensible job changes if any. It's all right to announce a disorder-but you can still do so as long as the events are relatively regulated (and in this everybody's different). Small achievements are just as important, just make sure that they are realistic and achievable at the time.

"Medication can help keep your moods on an even keel, but it is trial and error."

I had to live with the disease for almost 11 years before I found the right medication to keep my episodes safe, and my moods stabilized correctly. Once I got the mismedicine, I experienced severe depression and psychotic spells.

Mood stabilizers like lithium can really help. My longtime mood stabilizer Carbamazepine stopped holding me, and I became aggressive as I transformed from an adolescent into an adult. Make sure you talk about the right medicine for your doctor and don't be scared of medications like lithium— my life has been saved.

All are testing, and error and a combination of antidepressants or anti-psychotics may be necessary. All these drugs have side effects, but if it significantly helps your mental health, just make sure that you do so under the guidance of a psychiatrist.

"You can live and live well."

In 2014 I was treated and very depressed for a severe manic episode. It took me one and a half years to recover from the damage. Nevertheless, I have been volunteering with mental health organizations following rehab and started a book Be Ur Own Light (www.beurownlight.com) about mental health stigma, and writing Rethink Mental Health, Time to Transform, Bipolar Great Britain and other websites such as the Huffington Post UK. You can survive. You will live. Yes, you may have other problems with mental health (I have anxiety), but you can still achieve what you want, whether large or small. Live your dreams. Live your dreams.

When you are initially diagnosed with or accused of a depressive disorder because of your behavior and signs, you can be confused and exhausted. Day by day, the most important thing to do is to get the right support. It is not necessary to live a painful, diminished existence but with the correct medications, counseling, and support networks, including good medical staff.

Problems can sound boring and scary. But you can step into the sun. Be kind to you. Be kind to you. The illness isn't the owner, and you can heal once more. I wish I knew this when my journey started and what I wanted to share with you.

Jeanette's story

Jeanette is depressive with antidepressants since she was 18. Her birth was unplanned, and she was extremely anxious because it was said that getting pregnant and consuming lithium was very harmful.

I learned I was expecting when I was home for 11 weeks. I shouldn't get pregnant because I was on bipolar lithium disorder. I was really nervous and anxious, and I quickly phoned the doctor and said lithium in weeks 1–4 was most risky, so I couldn't stop taking it. I didn't think the kid was going to be all right. People gave me all those numbers, but I didn't truly accept it in my head.

At first, I was really afraid to lose the baby, but as it went further, something was wrong.

Around 22 weeks, I had to have another MRI to check at the heart chambers because lithium might damage the heart, so I was really terrified. I really didn't think I should give birth to a happy baby who'd thrive. "Jeanette had to struggle with her boyfriend's split, too, because he didn't want the child. Through her birth, her family and friends, and a perinatal therapist, a perinatal group counselor and a consultant sister helped her tremendously.

Although she suspected herself of having been pregnant while on lithium, she never felt criticized by experts.

I thought people might not encourage me because I had made a dumb mistake of getting pregnant with lithium, but I never felt that way.

Try to remain optimistic and accept the assistance that you get. Nobody will ever make you feel bad for wondering if you are nervous. If you compete alone and don't let people know, they can't help you, but if you let people know that you need more assistance, they are more than happy to give it to you in my experience.

When she was 40 weeks old, Jeanette was so concerned that the doctor decided to reassure her whether the infant was OK.

Her baby was born healthy. Unfortunately, her perinatal psychiatrist, midwife, and CPN were all on leave, and she became very unwell when she was not given the right medication.

There was a lot of work because I didn't sleep, so once I had the kid, I didn't sleep, so I was a little nervous." I got drugs, so they didn't be good enough because my psychiatrist didn't give them to me. I thought I was going crazy because I realized I had taken it, but that female with a dress and a white coat insists that I did not. I ended up spending a couple of days at the mental Mother and Baby Clinic. I get very weak with the depression when I'm getting low, and I was really afraid I couldn't produce a drink, I couldn't bathe him, change my nappy. It was so terrifying to me how I was going to handle this. "Jeanette felt easily stronger once at home and back on lithium.

"Everything turned out to be ok given my concern about the health of the baby, and I'm now only one mother to a lovely 18-month-old and indeed very satisfied."

Suzy's Story

Most people know me in track and field as a 3-time Olympian. And as my sporting journey began in my teens, in 2005, a year after my graduation, my personal journey began with mental illness.

I was the proud mother of a beautiful baby girl, but I looked for treatment for post-partite depression and anti-depressants were prescribed.

Quick forward until March 2011. My daughter was 6, and suddenly I stopped taking my anti-depressants (I never thought much about the side effects). In a few hours, I was once again discouraged and became suicidal. In turn, my 20-year engagement with my sweetheart college collapsed. Once, I've been looking for help, although it's not the last time.

I saw a general practitioner who could say I was obviously not good, and a new anti-depressant was prescribed. I was not listened to as a therapist, and my family history was not addressed when it came to mental illness (my uncle, as he went away from his medication, had bipolar disorder, died later of suicide). I could see this new medicine dragging me out of the gloom in a few hours. Ultimately, it worked miracles for me and made me feel better than before... or so I was told. I felt euphoric most of the time and wanted to live life to the fullest unexpectedly. I had stuff from the bucket list to carry on, and there were no inhibitions.

To hell in Wisconsin with my dull, "natural," worldly life.

What became apparent in weeks after I started this new drug was that I really wanted to have sex. I was always a physical person, but it was special-different. It was also obvious to me that in my marriage, I wouldn't get what I wanted.

So, I started taking lots of trips to Las Vegas in the next 6 months and soon started paying for sex. On quick trips to Las Vegas, my newly found destination, I would have multiple meetings with men and women that enhanced my senses. I'd come gradually up the ante. Threesomes. Threesomes. Public identity. And then, I had sex for money secretly. Seek danger, thrill, and tabus, and it's never been appropriate. I've been insatiable. I would be in a state half a morning marathon and fly to Vegas that evening to live my secret life as an escort. All that time in Wisconsin, my husband and daughter were back home. I will quickly become one of the most searched after escorts in Vegas, totally unfazed. I loved life, the rush, I felt it could last forever. But after a year, my secret life was revealed to the nation. My life was ruined.

My new life has been taken away from me. I was scared my family and friends would give me up. I felt that nothing was wrong with me, but everyone around me insisted and asked me to find help. If I had any chance to keep my baby, I realized I had to satisfy. So I've been looking for support, but not because I felt I needed it, but because I felt I needed to help someone in order to get them out of my back and return to my glorious life in Vegas.

While trying my best to taunt a doctor, he diagnosed me with bipolar disorder.

I was wondering, are you serious? He said hypersexuality, irrational thinking, and bizarre behavior. Yes, I was thinking. I like sex, and in my life, I finally discovered my love and intent. But the reality exploded in my stomach–and my lengthy, frustrating road to recovery was just starting, but I didn't know it at the time. Luckily, my result was good, and I want to keep it that way. This took a very long time to return. There have been many losses.

The road to wellness is not smooth, and early recovery was the hardest period I have ever experienced. Today, however, I can reflect and share lessons learned.

And one of them would certainly relate to age and to mental illness. How do I recognize what is and is not safe sex? Which red flags will I look for?

Psychological and mental illness is indeed a complicated relationship, and I'm clearly the poster child. Hypersexuality is a very true, fairly constant, yet underestimated bipolar disorder symptom. This isn't just an elevated sex drive for hypersexuality. It's life in overdrive–sex thought dominates you. Gender becomes the number one goal in your life, regardless of what you normally do. Thinking rationally comes out, and thrill / risk is an impulse. You focus solely on the moment. The consequences of your subconscious are the last thing.

Around 50% of those dealing with bipolar disorder report hypersexuality as a symptom, but when it comes to bipolar disorder, I've found sex is some kind of final frontier. No one wants to talk or discuss it. Most workers with mental health struggle with how to cope with it.

CONCLUSION

Perhaps one of the oldest known diseases is bipolar disorder. Research shows that early medical records describe some of the signs. It was first identified in the second century. Aretaeus of Cappadocia (a city in ancient Turkey) first recognized some of the symptoms and felt that they could be related. His observations were not noted or substantiated until, in 1650, the book The Anatomy of Melancholia, published by a scientist named Richard Burton directly on depression. Many in the area of mental health tend to use his results today, and he is considered to be the founder of depression as a mental illness.

In 1854 Jules Falret invented "circular foolishness" and made the connection between depression and suicide. His research contributed to the term bipolar disorder because he was able to distinguish between agitation and elevated moods. If he recognized as distinct from normal illness, and eventually, in 1875, his reported observations were named clinical manic-depressive psychosis. Another lesser-known fact attributed to Falret was that he found that in certain families, the disease seemed to be found, thus very early recognizing a genetic connection.

Francois Baillarger claimed that bipolar disorder and schizophrenia differed greatly. He characterized the disease's depressing process. This achievement caused bipolar syndrome to be identified by other mental disorders of that period. In 1913, the term manic-depressive was established by Emil Kraepelin with a detailed study of depression effects and a small portion of a manic state. In fifteen years, this mental illness method was fully accepted and became the dominant theory at the beginning of the 1930s.

In 1952, The Journal of Nervous and Mental Disorder published a bookthat looked at the biology behind the disorder and reported the possibility that manic depression was present in families already impacted by it. Most individuals with the condition have been institutionalized throughout the 1960s and have earned no financial support because the Senate refused to recognize manic depression as a genuine disease. It was only at the beginning of the 1970s that legislation and guidelines were introduced to help people impacted, and the National Association of Mental Health (NAMI) was established in 1979.

By 1980, bipolar disorder (1980) became a medical word for manic depressive disorder contained in the American Psychiatric Association's Medical and Statistical Manual (DSM-III). In the 1980s, a study was first able to differentiate between adult and adolescent bipolar disorder, and even still further studies are needed to determine the likely causes and alternative ways of treating the disease.